Brucey Gravy

Thomas F. Hall

Thomas F Hall

4th Printing

Pass the Gravy

You may be wondering about the title of this book and what it has to do with anything. Real Brucey gravy was very special to me as I was growing up. It made everything taste wonderful! I'd eat anything as long as it had Brucey gravy on it. Brucey gravy had a powerful influence on me.

Sometimes we do not realize the influential grip or impact we have on lives we encounter. It's kinda like Brucey gravy. As this gravy blanketed my potatoes and clung to my meat, it completely changed the flavor of things or simply enhanced it. Because there was an encounter, a change occurred.

Throughout my life many people have been like that special Brucey gravy for me. They've had a profound impact on my life and didn't even know it. The same is true of events and circumstances that happened along the way. Sometimes even Brucey gravy was hard to swallow.

So, that's what this book is about—strong influences and me growing up. It may seem to start out rather slowly, but stick with it. You'll be smothered with Brucey gravy by the time you finish!!

Please!

A special thanks to my wonderful wife, Sandy, whose hard work editing and faith in my writing style helped me to complete this book.

CONTENTS

My First Friend

ears welled up in my eyes and overflowed into a steady stream of water rolling down my cheeks. Dad's face was red as he hung up his razor strap, and so was my butt! I wanted to cry out but didn't utter a sound. I knew I deserved punishment for what I just put my parents through. Getting into trouble came quite naturally for me, and it started at a very young age.

I grew up playing in the streets, alleys, and parks close to my home in South Minneapolis. It was during the 1940's and 1950's when our country was rebounding from World War II. My father was a banker. My mother was a homemaker totally dedicated to her family. I was fortunate to have parents who loved each other and all their children deeply.

Dad was a strong man with a gentle nature. He stood five feet six inches tall, had a pot belly and balding gray hair, and wore glasses. A huge smile graced his face. He was extremely good natured and optimistic. People called him 'Happy Hall.' Dad radiated confidence and I loved being around him.

My father did not have a car. Everyday he rode the streetcar to work in the downtown area. I remember watching for him to come home at 5:30 each afternoon. Often I would see him, run into his arms, and walk with him to our house. He worked at Northwestern Bank as an auditor, so he only earned a moderate income. I remember the bank because it had a huge weather ball on top of it. I could see that weather ball all the way from Sibley

1

Park by my house. The weather ball turned three colors: red, green, and white. Red meant the temperature was going higher, green meant no change foreseen, and white as snow meant the temperature was going very low. If the ball was blinking, it meant there would be some form of precipitation. I always looked at the weather ball each night when I got older. I liked knowing about the weather and felt secure knowing my dad worked there. Dad was an intelligent man with only an eighth grade education. During the 1930's he was moving up the ladder of success at a different bank. When the depression hit, that bank was forced to close. Dad had to begin his career all over again and never rose above a bank auditor. In spite of this set back, Dad was content and had a good self-image. He was a good role model for me because of his strong character and cheerful nature.

In the morning I loved to watch my father shave. It was more of an art than a science to him. Dad would go into the bathroom wearing just his tee-shirt and underwear. His tee-shirt was the kind you see muscle men wear. It had thin little straps that draped over his shoulders. I could see Dad's big hairy chest and arms. As Dad rinsed his face with cold water, he made a loud blubbering sound. After drying his face with a towel, Dad wet a small brush with warm water and lathered it up with soap from a white jar. He brushed the soapy lather on his face, and it stuck to his stiff little whiskers. Next, he took his folded razor out of its plastic holder and flipped his wrist. The long shiny blade snapped out and locked into place. At the side of the sink hung a long strap made out of leather. Dad picked up this strap and moved the razor back and forth against it so fast I could barely see the blade. I only heard its rhythmic sound. I loved that sound as the blade slapped, slapped, slapped against the leather in a perfect beat. Then, Dad pulled a single hair from the side of his balding head and split it in half with the razor. The razor was now sharp enough to take the whiskers off his face. Dad began to shave by carefully removing the lather from the side of his temple. He stretched his skin and made very clean cuts with each stroke. He moved to his upper lip, down to his chin, and over to the left side of his face. It was like watching a master craftsman. Finally, Dad removed the lather from his neck with fine long strokes. He ended this experience with a splash of warm water, a gentle drying with a clean towel, and a final slap of after-shave lotion. I share this experience with you because it fascinated me, and I wondered if I could ever master this skill as an adult. Also, that razor strap played a significant role in my life.

My family eventually grew to seven children, six boys and one girl. Because it was so large, I only knew my father from a distance. Dad was never able to spend much time with us kids individually. Although we were never very close, I loved and respected him very much. I am the third oldest. My brother, David, was seven years older than me and my sister, Gwen, five years older. Needless to say, I didn't get much attention from them. David wanted me to be tough, so he wrestled and punched me a lot. Gwen did spend some time with me and usually treated me well. Mom, however, was always around.

Mother was a dynamo! She was full of energy and lived for her kids. She did not work outside the home and was always there for us when we needed her. She was five feet three inches tall, had sparkling blue eyes, and wore glasses. She was outgoing and always busy. Deeply religious, Mom made church, prayer, and Bible reading a regular part of our family time. I loved Mom deeply but did not openly show her affection.

Early on I was a little boy on the move who loved action and excitement. At first Mom only let me play in our backyard, which had a white picket fence around it. However, much of Mom's energy was spent looking for me when the gate was left open. Perhaps that's how I met my first neighborhood friend. Bruce Wakefield and I discovered each other early in life. It was before we started in school, somewhere between the ages of three and four. He quickly became my constant companion.

Bruce lived across the alley from me and a couple houses down. His father was a huge man about six feet two inches tall and weighed about two hundred sixty pounds. As a songwriter and a bandleader, he wasn't home much and seemed to take very little interest in his children. Bruce had a younger sister who was quiet and a loner. His mother worked outside the home as a secretary, so he had a babysitter during the day. Not too many mothers worked outside the home in the 1940's, so this was rather unusual. His mom was devoted to her children, however, and treated me very warmly. Bruce's family structure and atmosphere were completely different from mine. Although I didn't really notice this until we got older, it did have a profound impact on the course our lives took.

I remember an incident in our early years I will never forget. At the ripe age of four and a half, Bruce peddled down the alley and into my driveway on his tricycle. He was obviously upset about something.

"Bruce, what's the matter?"

"My parents are mean and I'm running away! Do you want to go with me, Tommy?"

"Sure," I said.

I got my tricycle and we both peddled down the alley, which had a small hill at the end going to Forty-Second Street. This was a busy street with lots of traffic and streetcar tracks. The busiest streets in the 1940's had streetcar tracks on which electric street-cars carried people all over the city. They were like big buses. These streetcars had long antennas which hooked to electric wires overhead. The wires propelled the streetcars when the switch was thrown by the conductor.

"Brucey?"

"What, Tommy?"

"My parents said I could never cross Forty-Second Street."

"'Okay," Bruce yelled. "We'll just stay on this side of the street!"

So, the two of us peddled down the sidewalk going from block to block as we ran away from home. It was about eleven o'clock in the morning on a warm summer day. We reached Twenty-Eighth Avenue, which was a busy intersection with a traffic light. There were stores and buildings on each corner. I especially remember Scott's Drug Store where Bruce's dad took us for a malt or a cherry coke occasionally.

"I know where we are, Bruce. There's Scott's Drug Store."

"Yup," he said confidently. "And, I know exactly where we are going!"

We had been peddling for about two hours when we came to a railroad track. There were two big iron rails with railroad ties laid underneath them. The large wooden ties were flush to the ground with crushed rocks pressed flat between them.

"Let's go down the middle of these tracks, Tommy," Bruce said.

" Okay. It should be fun," I responded.

These railroad tracks were active, and trains traveled down them daily. However, down the the middle of these tracks we peddled, oblivious to any danger that might come up. Bruce was out in front of me and got farther and farther ahead. Finally, he got so far ahead I could barely see him. I began to get frightened and stopped. Bruce never looked back and kept on going until he was out of my sight. He thought I was right behind him. I didn't know what to do. I was alone now, frightened, and beginning to panic. I thought I would never get home again and was sorry I ran away. I didn't know where I was or what to do. I felt helpless and sat on my tricycle and sobbed and sobbed. Finally, Bruce realized I wasn't with him. He turned around, came back, and found me crying.

"What's the matter, Tommy?" he asked empathetically.

"I'm scared, Bruce! Do you know where we are?"

"Sure I do!".

"I want to go home, Bruce! Will you take me home?" I whined.

"Okay, Tommy, follow me!"

"Bruce?"

"Yes, Tommy?" he responded.

"Please don't go so fast cuz I can't keep up with you," I pleaded.

"Okay."

The two of us headed back down the railroad tracks towards home. I trusted Bruce and just knew he could get us home. It's remarkable how he always gave me confidence when I was with him. After much peddling, we finally reached Forty-Second Street. We pulled our tricycles over the tracks, got on the sidewalk, and began the long ride to our houses. We were still about a mile away. I was tired and hungry but just kept following Bruce. Finally, we made it back to Twenty-Eighth Avenue. This was the same busy intersection with stores, a gas station, and buildings on each corner. I just couldn't hold my emotions inside any longer and began to cry and cry.

"What's the matter now, Tommy?" Bruce asked.

"I'm hungry, Brucey!"

We parked our tricycles next to Scott's Drug Store, and Bruce told me to sit on the sidewalk and wait for him. I watched as he walked into the store and wondered what he was going to do. I remember seeing him disappear into the store and looking up at all the big adults. All I could see were their legs, and then I lost sight of Bruce. After a little while he came out with a bag of Planter's Peanuts.

"Where did you get the peanuts?"

"On one of the shelves!"

Bruce poured half of the bag of peanuts into my hand, and he took the other half. We sat there eating those wonderfully scrumptious tasting peanuts. Then, with a full tummy and my confidence in Bruce totally restored, we continued on our journey. It was beginning to get dark as we approached our neighborhood. We had been gone for about six hours. When we came within a block of our houses, a neighbor rushed up to us.

"Where have you boys been?" she asked. "The whole neighborhood is looking for you and so are the police!"

When I heard the word police, I began to cry. She took us to our homes. I walked into my house and saw a terrified look on Mom's face. When she saw me, she began to cry. Then I heard her say, "Thank the Lord! My prayers have been answered!"

I told Mom the whole story. Mom and Dad talked it over and told me I was a bad boy and needed to be disciplined! Dad gave me three swats with the razor strap. As the leather slapped against my bare bottom, tears welled up in my eyes. It was like a thousand bees stung me at once, but I didn't cry out. I knew what I did was wrong. When it was over, I went to my room. Eventually the pain subsided, but that wasn't the worst of the discipline. I was grounded and couldn't see Bruce for a whole week.

After the week had ended, I went over to Bruce's house. I rang the doorbell, and Bruce came to the door.

"Can you come out and play?"

"Sure," he said.

"I don't think I'm going to run away again, Bruce."

"I'm not either," he responded.

"My dad spanked me with the razor strap and then grounded me for a whole week."

"That's nothing, Tommy! My dad sat on me and he weighs three hundred pounds!"

Bruce continually sought out adventure. He showed no fear in trying new things and appeared very confident. Although mellow, he desired to fulfill his boundless energy with some form of action. We looked odd together with his dark skin and black hair and my very light skin, blond hair, and blue eyes. After we discovered each other, we wanted to be together continuously. We were always asking our parents to be at each other's houses. We just seemed to click! I adored Bruce! He could do no wrong in my sight. I wanted to not only to be with him but be like him. I wanted to talk the way he did and walk the way he did. This friendship deepened and grew until our teenage years.

Brucey and Tommy — friends.

A New Beginning

Bruce and I began school in the fall of 1946. We were enrolled at Miles Standish Elementary School in the afternoon kindergarten class. This was a new experience for us because we used to have free reign of our neighborhood and weren't used to sitting very long in one place. Kindergarten wasn't bad because we did a lot of fun things like block building and finger painting. The worst, however, was nap time. We had to bring a little rug to school and rest on it for fifteen minutes. That time seemed like an eternity to two active little boys. We couldn't wait for school to end so we could play in the neighborhood again.

First grade was a real shock! The teacher wanted us to sit in a desk and learn to read. That was a difficult task for the two of us because there wasn't enough action and we needed to be on the move. We barely made it to lunchtime when we got to go home for an hour. Bruce always came home with me because his mom was working. Mom would fix soup and sandwiches for us.

I also remember third grade. That's when Bruce had another bright idea which got us both into a lot of trouble. It was in the fall. This season in Minnesota was breathtaking! The leaves turned colors and reds, yellows, golds, and greens filled your vision as you looked to the sky. Your nostrils also filled with the scent of brisk fresh cool air in the morning. Bright azure sky sparkled during the day, and cool crisp evenings tingled your spine. As neighbors burned their leaves, the air filled with a special aroma. An aura of excitement permeated the air because summer had ended, school had started, and the football season had begun. I've always liked this time of year because people are energetic and active. One clear sunny October day, Bruce came to my house to pick me up for school the way he usually did. I met him in my driveway.

"I'm not going to school today. I'm playing hooky!" Bruce stated.

"What's hooky?" I inquired.

"That's when you skip school and just have fun. Do you want to play hooky with me?" he asked.

"Sure," I said. I usually went along with everything Bruce wanted to do. He had a great influence over me! We headed toward school but then veered off in another direction.

"So, what do we do now?" I asked.

"Well, we can't go back to our neighborhood or your mom will see us. Let's just walk around and find something to do."

We walked through alleys feeling kind of guilty for not going to school, but neither of us said anything to each other. Finally, we found a driveway where some kids had left little trucks in the dirt. We sat down and played with the trucks. We built roads, had races, and just passed the time, which moved ever so slowly, until we were totally bored.

After we were through playing, we went to Henry's Grocery Store. This was a store at the end of the block in our neighborhood where our parents bought all our groceries. It was a white building with a flat roof and was about the size of two homes. Inside the store was a checkout counter with a cash register and a rack with books of customers. One book had the name Hall and another one had Wakefield. Both of our parents charged their groceries and then paid Henry at the end of the month. Behind the counter were all kinds of penny candy which Bruce and I bought all the time. Henry and the butcher, Mr. Olson, knew us very well. They liked us and treated us very kindly. There were aisles with food, a freezer section, and a butcher shop in the back of the store. We often went there to buy candy and popsicles. When we walked into the store, Henry asked us why we weren't in school.

I said, "The teacher let us out early because we had a doctor's appointment."

As I lied, my ears turned red. I could never lie very well, and

Henry gave me a strange look. I think he knew I was lying.

"Well, you'd better get home then."

We looked at the clock. It was still an hour before lunch. We knew we couldn't go home yet or we would get caught. So, we just walked around the neighborhood totally bored. It's amazing how slow time moves when you want it to go fast. Finally, we went home for lunch.

"How was school this morning, Tommy?" Mom asked.

"It was okay."

"What did you do today?" she asked.

"Not much, just read and did a little arithmetic. You know, Mom, the same old thing," I said trying to act casual.

I glanced at Bruce, and he looked kind of scared. My ears were red and my face was flushed. I sure didn't like lying to Mom, but what else could I do? She didn't question me any further and, thank goodness, dropped the subject.

On our way to school in the afternoon, we both realized we needed an excuse. Our third grade teacher, Mrs. Anderson, was very strict and a strong disciplinarian. She also lived in our neighborhood only about a block from our houses.

"What are we going to tell Mrs. Anderson?" I asked Bruce.

"Tell her we had to go to the dentist and our moms forgot to write a note."

"You mean tell her we both had a dentist appointment on the same day?" I asked.

"Yes! She knows we're neighbors and my mom works. We'll just tell her our moms made us both appointments on the same day. She'll never suspect a thing, Tommy! Just trust me, okay?" he pleaded. "And no matter what happens, Tommy, stick to the same story. Because if one of us changes it, we'll get caught and be in big trouble!" Bruce stated forcefully.

"Okay, I promise," I said. I always kept my promises to Bruce.

When we got to school, Mrs. Anderson asked us where we were that morning. We told her we had dentist appointments and our moms forgot to write us a note.

She looked at us very sternly and said, "Are you sure?"

"Oh yes, we're sure," we said hesitantly.

"Bruce, I want to talk with you alone in the cloakroom!" said Mrs. Anderson harshly.

The cloakroom was in the back of the classroom where we

hung up our coats. They were in there for about ten minutes. I went to my seat. I was very worried but remembered my promise to Bruce. I would stick to my story no matter what happened. I was determined not to break down because of my promise to Bruce.

After Mrs. Anderson and Bruce came out of the cloakroom, she called me in there. I was so scared that I couldn't even look at Bruce. She asked me again where I was that morning. I told her the same story. I was frightened and hated to keep on lying, but I couldn't change the story because I would get Bruce in trouble. Finally, she said in a loud stern voice, "Tommy, you are lying! Bruce told me the truth! He said you both played hooky this morning. Because he told me the truth and you kept on lying, your punishment will be more severe! Do you understand?" she shouted.

"Yes, ma'am," I responded.

I couldn't believe Bruce broke. I felt betrayed, hurt, and deeply frightened because of the severe punishment I was going to receive. I felt angry that I would be punished more severely than Bruce when it was all his idea. I walked back into the classroom and glared at Bruce! He looked back at me sheepishly.

Mrs. Anderson called my mom and told her the whole story. Mom said she was more disappointed in my lying than skipping school. Dad spanked me with the razor strap. I can remember him saying, "This hurts me more than it hurts you, Son." I don't think he could feel the sharp stinging sensation I was feeling on my butt at the time he said that. Later on in life, I remembered that statement and understood what he meant. Dad didn't want me to grow up to be a liar. I was also grounded for two weeks, which I hated even more.

I was really mad at Bruce! I wouldn't walk to school with him or even speak to him. This was the first time he really let me down. I was hurt and angry. I thought our friendship was over!

Finally, Bruce came to me and said, "Tommy, can we talk?"

"What's there to talk about? You're a fink!" I stated nonchalantly. That was hard for me because I had never been angry or even disappointed with Bruce before.

He kept persisting and finally I said, "Okay."

He told me his side of the story. He said Mrs. Anderson knew he was lying and told him if he would tell her the truth, the punishment would be less severe.

"I had to tell her because she wouldn't let up. When she called you into the cloakroom, you wouldn't even look at me. I'm sorry, Tommy! Please forgive me and be my friend again," Bruce pleaded. "You're my best friend in the whole world, and I don't like us not talking to each other. Please, Tommy, please forgive me," he continued.

What could I do? Bruce wanted to make up, and I was miserable.

"Okay, Bruce, I forgive you," I said as we shook hands and made up.

Bruce and I did have our differences later on when we got older. However, this was the only time in our young childhood when we were separated for any long period of time.

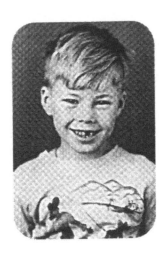

Summer Vacation

During the summer our neighborhood came alive with activities. There was always something going on. The weather turned warm and everything in nature seemed to turn a deep green. Lawns were thick and lush, and the trees were covered with leaves. I loved to lay on my back in our yard and look up at the soft blue sky with the white billowy clouds gently rolling by. The air smelled sweet and fresh. As I deeply inhaled, my lungs would expand and feel like cool water entering a parched stomach after a long dry spell. Laying there, watching nature, and totally absorbed with the beauty around me, I heard Bruce's welcomed voice calling to me one summer day.

"Hey, Tommy! Do you want to go swimming?"

I sat up and saw him coming through our gate with his swimming suit on, his tennis shoes on his feet, and a towel hanging around his neck. Bruce and I had expanded our neighborhood territory. We were now allowed to go to Lake Hiawatha and swim in the little wading pool. This park was only two blocks from our house. We had a ball swimming in this little pool.

"My mom said we could go to Lake Nokomis and swim at the big beach," Bruce announced.

"Are you kidding?" I questioned because Lake Nokomis was about a mile away. We had never been allowed to go that far alone before. "I don't think my mom will go for it, Brucey!"

"Just tell her you'll be with me and there is a lifeguard on duty all the time. It's perfectly safe. Besides, my mom said she would drive us there and pick us up in a couple of hours."

"Okay, I'll try to convince Mom, Bruce, but don't hold your breath."

"Mom, can Bruce and I go swimming at Lake Nokomis this morning?" I asked.

"Certainly not, Tommy. That lake is too far away!"

"Bruce's mom said she would drive us there and pick us up when we're done in a couple hours," I said trying to sound as calm and convincing as possible.

"I'm sorry, Son. That lake is just too far away for you two boys to be going all alone."

"Please, Mom," I pleaded. "The pool is just too small for us to have any fun anymore. Besides that, there is a lifeguard at the beach all the time, Mom. All our friends from school go there, Mom. Please let us go! We'll be all right! I promise! Bruce is outside right now with his bathing suit on. We'll be all right, I promise!"

"Are you sure his mom said she would drive you?" she asked hesitantly.

I could tell she was beginning to soften and really began laying it on. "Mom, all the kids from school go there and really have a good time. You can call their parents if you don't believe me. Mom, I'm growing up and you've got to begin to let go a little," I said trying to sound convincing.

"So, you think you're a big boy now! Well, let me tell you something, Son! You're only ten years old and have a lot more growing up to do before you can go just anywhere you want. Do you understand?" she said firmly.

Oops! Maybe I pushed a little too hard, I thought. Now I'll have to soften her up a bit. "Mom, I know I'm just ten and have a lot to learn from you and Dad. I just think it's time I should be allowed to go swimming with Bruce. That's all!"

"Well, I'll call Mrs. Wakefield and see what she thinks."

"Gee, thanks, Mom! You're the best Mom in the whole world," I said as I ran out the door to tell the good news to Bruce.

Bruce was patiently waiting outside the door listening to the whole conversation. "Did you hear that, Bruce? I didn't think I was going to make it for awhile there! Did you?"

"You should have heard yourself! You could have won an Academy Award for that performance," chuckled Bruce. Then, he gazed into space and thought deeply and stated seriously, "You know, Tommy, your mother really loves you. I can tell just by the way she talks and is so concerned about you. You're really lucky, you know, to have a mother like that. I just told my mom I was going swimming at Lake Nokomis and she said, 'Fine.'"

Bruce's mom drove us to the beach that afternoon. We waved good-bye as she drove away. We walked through the beach house where people showered and changed clothes after their swim. We stepped down the front steps and onto the concrete walkway in front of the building. There were people everywhere. Some teenagers were doing gymnastic tricks on the parallel and high bars. Some little kids were swinging very high on huge swings. To the right was a small building where refreshments were sold to hungry swimmers. A huge sand beach with a small lifeguard tower in the middle stretched out before us. A lifeguard sat on top of the tower. He was very tan and muscular, and his nose was painted white. Little kids were splashing in the shallow water, which was marked by posts with a large rope tied around them. Beyond the ropes lay a large flat dock with diving boards on each end. The bigger kids were jumping and diving off of it. A lifeguard sat in a small row boat between the ropes and the dock. Farther out in the lake stood a large tower about twenty feet high. On the beach people were laying on towels and blankets all over the place. Bruce and I looked for a spot to lay our blankets and take off our clothes. Everything, that is, except our swimsuits!

"Hey, this is great, Tommy! We're going to have a ball!" Bruce yelled as he ran for the lake. "Last one in is a rotten egg!" Then, I saw him disappear under the water.

I was a little more reluctant. But eventually, Bruce and I were having a riot diving under each other's legs and standing on our hands under water.

"Let's swim out to the end of the ropes, Tommy."

"Isn't it kind of deep out there, Bruce?"

"Not really! It's only up to our necks," he said as he began swimming toward the end of the ropes. I watched him swim and wondered where he learned because he never had lessons. The only swimming he'd ever done was in the wading pool with me. I followed Bruce out and had to stand on my tiptoes because the water was up to my chin. We were standing on the rope and diving off of it when Bruce got another bright idea.

"Let's swim out to the dock," he said. Without any hesitation, Bruce began swimming in water way over his head. I tried to follow but soon realized I couldn't swim that far and turned back. I watched as he swam with the confidence of a naval seal swimmer heading straight for the flat dock. His natural athletic ability and confidence amazed me. Everything seemed to come so easy for him, and he had no fear! The dock was about fifty yards from the ropes. Bruce had no problem reaching it safely. He took a few dives off the dock and waved to me as I watched him. Then, I saw Bruce look at the large tower which was another sixty yards farther out in the lake. I couldn't believe it when he dove off the flat dock and headed for the tower. I admired his courage and natural ability! When Bruce reached the tower, he looked a little winded and stayed at the bottom of the tower for a long time. Then suddenly, he began climbing the large tower. About half-way up he stopped and looked down. There were other swimmers climbing below him, so he had to continue on up the ladder. Finally, he made it to the top. I wanted to yell to the lifeguard to go get him because he was so young. But, I didn't. Bruce walked out to the end of the board and looked down. I know he wanted to go back down the ladder, but people were waiting to jump. Finally, he took a deep breath and off he went. What a dare devil! I couldn't believe it. I watched as Bruce entered the water. He seemed to be under for quite awhile. But finally, up he came. He headed straight back for the ladder and up he went again. Once he got the hang of it, there was no stopping him. He stood on the ladder and jumped and waved to me in the air as he was going down. He finally got tired and swam back to shore where I was waiting for him. Later, after I learned how to swim, Bruce and I spent many hours at the beach swimming to the dock and out to the tower.

We were an even funnier looking pair in the summer. Bruce got very very dark with his shinny black hair, and I hardly tanned but my hair bleached out into a bright blond color. We looked as different as night and day, but we were buddies.

Mr. Beckworth

Minneapolis is really an attractive city. Located in the Mid-Western part of the United States, it's filled with lakes, trees, creeks, and the Mississippi River. I lived at 4142 - 25th Avenue South and Bruce lived at 4151-24th Avenue South. There were about twelve houses on each side of a block separated by an alley with single unattached garages next to the alley. The side of the houses with the alley and garages were backyards. In front large elm trees on the boulevards formed an archway over the street. This archway was like a tunnel of living greenery in the summer. Sidewalks and curbs also ran parallel to the narrow streets. The houses were well kept with neat lawns, trees, bushes, and usually a garden. 4142 was a small white stucco house with two bedrooms downstairs and one large room upstairs which Dad fixed-up for us boys to sleep in. The alleys, yards, and street were my playground.

Our neighborhood was like one big happy family. After school all of the neighborhood kids met in the alley behind my house to plan things to do. Bruce and I expanded our friendships. Now we did things with Larry, Jimmy, Mike, Gary, and Allen. We were not involved in any organized activities yet, so we made up our own games! Kick the Can, Captain May I, Sardines, and Capture the Flag were some of our favorites. We also played war games. In order to play war, each of us made our own rubber gun. One season nobody made a finer gun than Bruce and me, thanks to Mr. Beckworth. It took us about a week to make these things of beauty.

"Tommy, let's make our rubber guns for the neighborhood war next week," said Bruce as he opened the gate to my backyard.

"Where are we going to get the wood this year, Bruce?" I responded.

"Mr. Beckworth is always working in his garage making something out of wood. I bet he'd have some good pieces for us."

"Hey! That's a great idea! Let's go talk to him right now."

We went down the front steps of my house, cut across a neighbor's yard, and walked down the alley toward Mr. Beckworth's garage. Mr. Beckworth's garage door was open, and he was inside working on a project on his wood turning lathe. Mr. Beckworth was thin, wore glasses, had gray hair on the side of his head and a bald spot in the middle, and he usually wore bib overalls with a white tee-shirt.

"Hi, Mr. Beckworth! Do you mind if we watch you for awhile?" asked Bruce.

"No, I don't mind. Come on in boys. I could use some company."

We often went to talk with Mr. Beckworth, and he seemed to like our company. He always seemed to have a smile on his face and enjoyed working in his homemade shop. He loved to talk, answer our questions, and give us advice. We visited his shop about once a week during the summer months. We were friends, and we always felt better after talking with him. It was really neat to have a friend like Mr. Beckworth.

"What are you working on, Mr. Beckworth?" I asked.

"I'm making a table for one of my kids. These will be the legs of the table." There was a piece of maple wood in the lathe that was being shaped into a leg with curves and designs on it. We knew it was maple because Mr. Beckworth taught use how to identify all kinds of wood by their color and the grain that ran through them. Underneath the lathe were wood shavings and sawdust. His garage was full of tools, machines, projects, and a variety of different kinds of wood. It smelled like fresh cut wood and had a varnish odor in the air.

"What are you boys up to today?" he asked.

"We were wondering if you had a nice piece of wood for us to make a rubber gun?" Bruce asked.

"Well, let me see," he said as he rummaged through his pile of scrap wood. "What size are you looking for?"

"Oh, I don't know. Maybe about the size of a gun barrel and handle," I stated.

"Just how are you boys going to make a rubber gun anyway?"

"Well, Mr. Beckworth, we get two pieces of wood and nail them together. One piece is longer than the other, so one looks like the barrel and the other looks like the handle. Then we take a clothespin, you know the kind with the spring that Mom uses to hang the wash, and we take it apart. It comes apart, you know! We nail half the clothespin to the handle, and then we hook it back together again."

Mr. Beckworth listened to Bruce intently, like Bruce was telling him about some new invention or something. His eyes were fastened on Bruce, and his forehead was wrinkled up like he couldn't believe what Bruce was telling him.

Bruce went on, "Now that the clothespin is attached to the handle and put back together again, it can open and close. The clothespin serves as the trigger. Next, we go get an old inner tube from Mr. Slip down at the gas station. We cut the inner tube into thin circular strips. We attach one end of the rubber strip into the clothespin and stretch the other to the end of the barrel. When we release the clothespin, the rubber comes flying off," Bruce said excitedly.

Mr. Beckworth just looked at Bruce with a puzzled look on his face.

"It really works, Mr. Beckworth!" I chimed in. "And if you want more power, you tie a knot in the rubber or maybe even two and stretch it a little tighter. Then, it really goes!"

"Yeah, and when you get hit, it kind of stings a little," Bruce added.

"Well, I'll be darned!" said Mr. Beckworth. "It sounds like you boys have a great idea!"

"It's not our idea. We've been having rubber gun fights in the neighborhood for years," Bruce stated nonchalantly.

"Let me see. I have some pine over here that might work just fine. If you boys want to, you can work right here in my shop. As a matter of fact, I would kind of like to see the finished product."

"Gee, thanks, Mr. Beckworth," we both said at the same time.

"We have to go now, but we'll be back tomorrow to begin working on our project," Bruce said.

"Thanks again for the wood," I added as we walked out of the garage and headed for home excited about our new project.

"Mr. Beckworth sure is nice, isn't he Bruce?"

"Yeah, I'm sure glad we got to know him, Tommy."

After a good night's rest, I went over to Bruce's house. He met me at the back door and said, "Let's call a neighborhood meeting. You take half the block, and I'll take the other half. We'll meet behind Henry's Grocery Store at 11:00 A.M. sharp."

At 11:00 o'clock everyone was there. Bruce began speaking, "We're going to have a rubber gun fight next Tuesday after lunch. We'll meet right here! You have about a week to make your guns, and you must supply your own rubbers. Are there any questions?"

"Yeah," said Larry. "What'll be the teams this year, Brucey?"

"Oh, I don't care as long as Tommy and I are on the same team!"

"That's not fair, Wakefield!" protested Mike. "You're always on the same team!"

"Too bad, Mike, but that's just the way it is! If you don't like it then you don't have to play."

"I wanna play, Bruce. I guess we can still pick fair teams anyway," Mike said.

"Sorry, but you guys know Tommy and I never split up!"

"Oh, all right," said Larry. "We'll all be ready with our rubber guns and here next Tuesday, Bruce."

After the meeting Bruce and I headed for Mr. Beckworth's garage. When we walked in, he greeted us with a smile. "I see you brought your wood," he said. "There's a little area over in the corner that I cleared off for you to work in."

"Thanks, Mr. Beckworth," we said.

"We have a week to make our guns before the neighborhood war begins," Bruce stated.

"Then you better quit standing around and get busy!"

"Okay," we said as we put the wood into the vice to nail it together.

"What are you doing?" asked Mr. Beckworth.

"We're nailing the wood together to make our gun," I stated with a puzzled look.

"Aren't you going to cut it out and sand it first?" he questioned.

"We've never done that before!" exclaimed Bruce.

"Well, boys," he said, "if you're going to do a job, you must do it right!"

"What do you mean, Mr. Beckworth?" I asked.

"I mean, if you're going to make a rubber gun, then don't just slop it together. Make the best rubber gun you can possible create! Be proud of what you do! No job is worth doing unless you do it well!"

"We don't know how to do it any other way," stated Bruce.

"Well, Mr. Beckworth, do you have any ideas?"

"Do I?" he said. "I thought you'd never ask!"

"You mean you would help us?" I said amazingly.

"No! This is your project and I won't help you. But, I will give you some ideas."

"What would you do, Mr. Beckworth?" I asked.

"I'd begin with a plan. Maybe I would work on the barrel first. I would file it down into a circle. Next, I would sand it until it was very smooth. I would then cut a handle into the correct shape. I would look at a real gun and make a pattern. I would figure out a way to attach the handle to the barrel without using nails."

"How would you do that, Mr. Beckworth?" asked Bruce.

"Good question, Brucey! And that's a good way to learn, ask good questions. I would drill out holes in the handle and make wooden pegs in the barrel. Then I would glue them together and sand it so well you couldn't see the seam."

"Wow! Mr. Beckworth, that's fantastic! Keep talking," I said excitedly.

"I would find some thin finishing nails and attach the clothespin to the handle. And if I wanted a double shooter, I'd make a wider handle and have one barrel on top of the other. Then, I could load up two rubbers at once."

"Mr. Beckworth, you're the smartest man in the world," said Bruce. "Do you really think we can do all that in a week?"

"That depends on how hard you want to work."

"Let's get going, Bruce!" I said.

For a week we worked on our rubber guns. We cut the wood, sanded, filed, and shaped our guns. We glued the handle to the barrel. We each made a double shooter. When we got stuck, Mr. Beckworth was right there to answer our questions, but he never did our work. When we were finished with our guns, we

21

put on two coats of varnish and one coat of wax. Our guns couldn't have looked any better than if they came off the shelves of Dayton's Department Store. We cut out some rubbers, tied them in a knot, loaded them up, and shot them at a target in Mr. Beckworth's backyard. They were perfect! Mr. Beckworth seemed to enjoy our new found success as much as we did. We thanked Mr. Beckworth and headed for home filled with pride because of our newly created treasures.

Mr. Beckworth taught us to be resourceful, ask questions, and work hard on anything that's worth doing. This knowledge helped me all my life. Not only that, Mr. Beckworth shared part of himself with two little kids. It wasn't until I was older that I fully appreciated what he did for Bruce and me that week. Mr. Beckworth was truly our friend!

The Rubber Gun Fight

It was a bright, sunny, summer morning when Bruce came over to my house with his new rubber gun. He knocked on my back door and said, "It's time to get ready for the neighborhood war, Tommy. Get your new gun, and let's go to the gas station and get some old inner tubes."

"I'll be right out, Bruce," I said as I excitedly ran up to my room and got my rubber gun.

We walked down to Slip's gas station hoping he'd have some old inner tubes for us. When we got there, Slip was under a car working on some brake pads.

"Hi, Slip," said Bruce. "Do you have any old inner tubes to spare for two rambunctious young boys?"

Slip slid out from under the car on his creeper and said, "Hi, Bruce. Hi, Tommy. What are you little munchkins up to now?" Slip was a man in his forties with black hair which was slightly gray around the temples. He always wore blue coveralls, and they were usually kind of dirty and greasy. He was about six feet tall and thin. Slip was friendly and outgoing. He loved to tease Bruce and me when we rode with our bicycles to his station from time to time. We formed a friendship with him, and he always seemed to have time for us.

"Slip, look at the rubber guns Bruce and I made," I stated excitedly.

His eyes lit up as he gazed on our newest creation. "Wow!" he exclaimed. "Did you guys make them by yourselves?"

"Well, to tell you the truth, Slip, we got a little help from Mr. Beckworth," said Bruce a little sheepishly.

"They're beautiful, guys! How do they work?"

"Well, Slip, that's what we need you for," I stated. "We need some old inner tubes. That is, if you have any. Then, we take a scissors and cut out a ring about a half inch wide. We attach one end of the ring into the clothespin and stretch the other over the barrel. When we release the clothespin, the rubber comes flying off."

"Yeah, and if we want it to go farther, all we have to do is tie a knot in the middle of the rubber and stretch it a little tighter. Then, it really goes far," Bruce chimed in.

"Well, I'll be darned. If that isn't a clever idea! Let me see if I have any old tubes for you guys." Slip went into the back room and came out with three old inner tubes and said, "How will these do?"

"They're perfect, Slip," said Bruce. "How much do we owe you?"

"No charge, guys. Now you go and have yourselves a good time."

"Gee, thanks, Slip," we said simultaneously.

We brought the tubes back to my house, went into the basement, and began to work. I ran upstairs and got my mother's good scissors. We cut out about twenty rubbers. Then, we loaded them on our guns and shot them at a box board target. We found we had to tie a knot and sometimes a double knot to stretch them tight enough to make them really fly. We had a mini-war game between ourselves and were fully satisfied with our new weapons.

"Well, Bruce, let's eat some lunch and go to Henry's Store and begin this neighborhood war."

"Sounds good, Tommy. We can eat at my house. I'll make some peanut butter and banana sandwiches." After sandwiches and milk, we headed for Henry's Store with our guns and ten rubbers each. As we neared the store, we saw the guys already gathering there.

"Hey, there comes Bruce and Tommy!" yelled Mike.

"Wow! Look at their guns," exclaimed Larry.

"Where did you get those guns?" blurted Mike. "And they're

double shooters too! That's no fair, Bruce," stated Mike harshly.

"Hey, we made these guns ourselves. No one said we couldn't have double shooters," responded Bruce. "If you don't like it, we'll forget it right now."

"Calm down, Bruce. We just wanted to know how you made them, that's all," said Mike softening his voice.

"Well, let's choose up sides, Mike," said Bruce who always seemed to be the one to get things going. "Since Tommy and I are on the same team, you can have the next pick, Mike."

"I should have the next two since you got to pick Tommy first," stated Mike. Mike Postello was our same age but much bigger than the rest of us. He was tough and feared no one except maybe Bruce. Bruce was the only one in the neighborhood who would stand up to Mike.

"Oh, all right, Mike! You take the next two picks," said Bruce. So Mike picked Larry and Allen to be on his side. That left us with Darryl, who was Allen's little brother.

"Okay, everyone gather around. The rules are the same as last year. Anyone who gets hit with a rubber is dead and out of the game. Is that clear? The team that has people still alive at the end of the game wins. The boundaries are the neighborhood block. Anyone who runs across the street is automatically out. We have one minute to hide and separate. Let the game begin and may the best team win!" yelled Bruce as we all scattered for cover.

Bruce, Darryl, and I met between two garages.

"Tommy, you cover my back side. Darryl, try to draw them out where we can get a shot at them because you're a pretty fast runner," Bruce instructed as we listened.

Suddenly, Mike appeared at one end of the garage. He pointed his gun at me and fired. I hit the deck just as the rubber flew over me .

"Run!" yelled Bruce. Darryl ran straight into Allen. Allen fired and hit Darryl. Just as Allen turned around, Bruce squeezed his clothespin and the rubber nailed Allen in the shoulder. Now, it was two against two. I tore down the alley with Mike hot on my heels. Bruce went after Larry.

As I was running, I saw a rubber fly over my head. I stopped because I knew Mike couldn't reload that fast and turned toward him. He was trying desperately to stretch his rubber on his gun as he saw me running at him. He loaded it just as I fired! My rubber went to his right. I then ducked behind a garage and tried circling around him. I didn't know where Bruce was, but I knew he was between Mike and me. I ran to the front of the block, hid behind some trees, and cautiously moved into the alley. Mike was nowhere in sight, which really bothered me. All of a sudden, Mike jumped out between two garages and startled me. He was right on top of me when he fired his rubber gun. The rubber just missed my left arm.

"I got you, Hall!" yelled Mike.

"No, you didn't!" I screamed back.

"You cheater!" yelled Mike as he tore after me. Mike was a fast runner and caught up to me with a flying tackle.

"You were hit, and I'm going to make sure you stay dead!" he screamed as he began throwing punches at my head. I couldn't throw him off of me because he was so big. So, I rolled over and covered up my head while he continued throwing punches at me. He was beginning to hurt me. I was getting scared because he seemed out of control.

In the meantime, Bruce had gotten Larry and was coming to help me out. When he saw Mike all over me, he came running and dove into him like a battering ram. Mike flew off of me and came to his feet. I got up and stood beside Bruce. "Come on, Mike! Now there's two of us for you to beat up," yelled Bruce.

Mike paused and said, "Bruce, I shot Tommy and he cheated!"

"The rubber missed me, Bruce," I stated.

"The game's over, Mike, and if you want any more, come on. Let's settle it right now!" glared Bruce.

"I'm not fighting both of you!" said Mike.

"You want one of us, you got both. Do you understand?" stated Bruce.

"I'm going home," said Mike. "I'm not playing with cheaters!"

Bruce and I turned and began to walk toward home.

"Thanks, Bruce! You saved my life! I was scared when he was beating on me. You came out of nowhere and got him off of me. You know, Bruce, he's really strong and kind of scary."

"You would have done the same for me, Tommy!"

"Just the same, Bruce, I owe you one."

"You owe me nothing! That's what friends are for."

Breaking Ties

Bruce and I had become very close friends. We did everything together. We slept over at each other's house two to
three times a week and ate meals together. Our families seemed
to encourage the deep bond developing between us. We also
began to notice the differences in our family structure.

Bruce's father was rarely home. When he was home, he
worked on writing songs with his piano and music note pad.
Totally absorbed in his work, he rarely noticed we were even in
the same room. We never interrupted or interacted with him.
Bruce wasn't a demanding child and didn't seem to need to
interact with his father. On the other hand, Bruce's mother was
very friendly and outgoing. She fixed us meals, and we talked
and laughed a lot together. She was very attractive with black
hair and dark silky skin. She enjoyed seeing us together and
drove us to many places and activities. Bruce's parents didn't
seem to have much in common and rarely did things together.

Because the atmosphere was so different at my house, Bruce
wanted to be over all the time. That was all right with me.
However, I did appreciate the peace and quiet at his home on
occasion. My family related completely different with many
activities, much interaction, and lots of humor. We were always
laughing at or with someone. We always ate the dinner meal
together too, and Bruce often joined us. My father began by
praying before we could start to eat. Sometimes I opened my
eyes and watched Bruce. He always closed his eyes and took this
part of the meal very seriously. This was different and special for

Bruce because his parents never said grace before eating. Our meal times were filled with laughter, stories, jokes, and pure enjoyment. Dad would tell a stupid joke like, "I buy all my ties in Connect-tie-cat." He then shut his eyes and laughed with such an infectious laugh that we all cracked up just watching him. Bruce would join in and be a part of my family. I could sense his excitement during these times.

Mom was a wonderful cook, and we never grew tired of her meals. She took pride in her cooking and felt satisfaction in watching the family. We not only enjoyed the food but got involved with the whole process that went along with eating together. It was a special time when we were really a family. We communicated and interacted like no other time during the day. Our evening mealtime was an adventure that energized me, not only physically but emotionally as well. Bruce did not have this experience with his family and loved this time as much or maybe even more than I did.

One evening we were all together sitting around our big oak table getting ready to eat a delicious meal Mom cooked for us. She served us mashed potatoes, meat, and vegetables. I loved mashed potatoes but hated gravy. Mom made thick dark brown gravy which I would never eat. That night Mom said, "Try some gravy, Tommy!"

"No thanks, Mom. I don't like gravy!"

"You know, Tommy, Bruce likes this gravy. In fact, it's his favorite!"

"He does? Put some on my potatoes, Mom."

I loved that gravy from that time on, and it became known as 'Brucey Gravy' in our home. To this very day, I never turn down this rich addition to my taste buds.

My parents deeply loved each other and were openly affectionate all the time. They would hug and kiss each other and us kids as well. This made an impact on both of our lives as we observed their love for one another.

Mom used to wash everybody's hair under the sink faucet every Saturday night. We didn't have showers in our home and really didn't even know what they were. Mom lathered up our hair with soap, massaged our scalp with her strong fingers, and rinsed the suds off with warm water. It felt so wonderful that I didn't want her to ever stop. I felt so clean and refreshed after she finished. I was truly ready for a good night's rest and church in the morning. When Bruce stayed over on Saturday nights, he received the same treatment. He felt the same way I did about the hair washing and scalp massage. After our shampoo, Dad cut our hair. This became a whole evening affair with our large family. Bruce seemed like part of my family. We were like brothers. We both noticed the great contrast in our family's lifestyles but never talked openly about it. It was sort of an unspoken rule between us.

My parents shocked me when I was ten years old. Our family had grown to nine members including my parents. We had outgrown our house and really needed a bigger one. My father announced he was going to put our house up for sale and find a larger one. I didn't want to move and leave the security of my old neighborhood. Our house sold quickly. We moved about a mile away into a four bedroom home next to an elementary school and a park. This move turned out to be perfect for my brothers and me, but at the time I wasn't thrilled about it. Our new house was about fifty years old and needed lots of work. It was a large two story house that provided the necessary space for our large family. Dad worked every spare minute on this house until it looked very attractive with a new paint job and new roof.

Bruce and I still attended the same elementary school even though we no longer lived in the same neighborhood. Somehow, we both sensed our friendship would never be quite the same. However, for eight years we shared a special, deep, impressionable friendship.

During the first three months in my new neighborhood, I longed to be back in my old, familiar surroundings. Mom allowed me to return to my old neighborhood on occasional weekends and spend time with Bruce. On one occasion, Bruce and I were having so much fun that I lost track of time. It got very late, so I called Mom and asked if I could stay overnight. She said no, and I was to come right home. It was dark and eerie out that night. I was frightened to walk home alone, but I didn't want to mention my fear to Mom.

I said good-bye to Bruce and began to run full-speed down the dark and dreary alley. Suddenly, I felt myself soaring through the air hearing a hissing, snarling sound. When I hit the concrete, I was bruised, frightened, and bewildered. I was also scared half to death! As I picked myself up and got my bearings, I discovered I had tripped over a cat. I decided running down alleys full-speed wasn't too smart, so I took a shortcut through the backyards. It was so black that I felt like I was in a tunnel twenty feet underground with no source of light. As I was running through the yard, my neck hit a clothesline and my feet kept going. Wham! Down I went again. Boy, this sure wasn't my night! I got up a little dazed with a stinging sensation on my neck. Then, I cut through another yard which had two large evergreen trees in it. I decided to run between the two trees. You guessed it! Down I went again tripping over a low wire fence between them.

By the time I arrived home, I was bruised, humiliated, and relieved all at the same time. I realized it was going to be much more difficult to spend time with Bruce in the future.

Mr. Capetz

"Hi, Tommy," said Bruce as we both met on the playground before school. It was the first day of fifth grade. "How do you like your new neighborhood?"

"It's okay, Bruce," I said, "but I miss all you guys in our old neighborhood! At least we're still going to the same school. Who do you think we'll get for a teacher this year, Brucey?"

"I don't know, Tommy, but I hope she's nice and not ninety-five years old."

"I know! It seems like all the teachers in our school have been around forever!"

"Well, let's go in and see who we have this year," said Bruce as we headed for the school doors. Our school was a two story, red, brick building. A fine lawn surrounded the building along with shrubs and trees. In back of the school was some playground equipment on one level and a playground area on another level surrounded by an iron railing on top of a concrete wall. Steps led down to the playground, which was largely a huge area of sand. On the far side of the playground was a huge chain link fence about ten feet high. The school and the playground took up a city block except for three houses still standing behind the chain link fence. We spent a lot of time playing all sorts of games on that playground during recess and after school. Bruce and I entered the building through two large doors with big brass handles on them. We walked through the hallways and up the stairway to the second floor.

"There's our new room, Tommy. Room 224," said Bruce as we

headed for our new home for another school year. We sat down and greeted old friends we hadn't seen all summer and waited for our new teacher. The bell rang and in walked an athletic looking young man. Bruce and I both sat up in our desks with our eyes wide open because we had never seen a man teacher. He walked to the front of the classroom with a huge smile on his face. This was also rather unusual for any teachers we had known. He was short and stocky, had black hair and a large forehead, and wore a blue suit with a white shirt and tie. His suit coat was unbuttoned, and his hands were in his pockets when he began speaking to us.

"Hi! My name is Mr. Capetz, and I'm going to be your teacher this year. I'm new to this school and, as a matter of fact, new to this profession. This is my first year as a classroom teacher, and you're going to be my very first class. My favorite subject is gym, so that's one subject we will never miss."

Bruce and I couldn't believe our ears. Bruce looked over at me and winked. Mr. Capetz was true to his word because we never did miss gym. In fact, that very first day he took us outside, and we played baseball. The girls played against the boys, and Mr. Capetz played for the girls team. He batted left-handed just to be fair, and I pitched to him. On the very first pitch I threw, Mr. Capetz hit the ball over the fence. Bruce and I knew right then we were going to have a very good year.

Bruce and I went to school early just to talk to Mr. Capetz. He was the first teacher who ever took a personal interest in us. In fact, once a week Mr. Capetz, Bruce, and I shot baskets down in the gym. He was the first teacher who I felt liked me and was in no way the least bit threatened by Bruce and me. Before that, we were considered discipline problems. Mr. Capetz loved his job and related very well to us kids. He even went to bat for us when we were wrong or got into trouble.

That happened in January when Bruce got another bright idea. And of course, I went along with it. Not only did I go along with it, I actually carried it out.

"Tommy, Tommy!" said Bruce very quietly while Mr. Capetz had his back to the class. "As soon as it's time for recess, grab your coat and run out to recess with me. Let's be the first ones out there!"

"Okay!"

When it was recess time, we both hurried to the cloakroom, grabbed our coats, and ran out for recess.

"Wanna have some fun, Tommy? Let's keep the kids inside and not let them come out for recess for awhile!"

"How are we gonna do that, Bruce?" I questioned.

"Do you see that broken hockey stick on the ground over there?"

"Yeah."

"Well, if we put it between the brass door handles, the doors won't open and no one can get out," said Bruce.

"Hey, that's a great idea!" I said as I ran for the broken hockey stick. I put the hockey stick between the large brass handles just as the kids were coming out for recess. What I didn't realize was that hockey sticks are made of hickory wood and very difficult to break. When the kids tried to open the doors, they bulged a little but the hockey stick held. More and more kids came, and soon they were all pushing at once. Bruce and I thought it was funny and began making faces and sneering at them. As more students came, the more frustrated they got because the door wouldn't open. They began to shout, "We want out! We want out!" The kids kept pushing, and the door kept bulging out each time they pushed.

All of a sudden there was a loud snap! One of the big brass handles broke! The brass handle came flying off, and all the kids piled out the door. Bruce and I took off running for the playground. After recess, we sheepishly went back to our classroom. Everyone in my classroom knew what I had done, but no one said anything to Mr. Capetz. At our school no one ever tattled, not even the girls. It was kind of an unwritten rule. If anyone did, they would hear about it in the cloakroom or out in the playground. The silence was broken when Miss Psalm's very strict principal voice came over the intercom. She said, "Someone has broken the brass handle off the school doors. It happened during recess! I want the guilty party to come to my office at once!"

My classmates looked at me, but I didn't budge. I looked over at Bruce. His dark face was white! He was shaking his head and mouthing the words, "No, No!"

About fifteen minutes later, I asked Mr. Capetz if I could go to the bathroom. As I was returning to my room, I saw Miss Psalm with a fourth grade girl going from class to class. I felt doomed because I knew they were looking for me. I went and sat in my seat and waited for judgment to fall. Finally, the door opened as Miss Psalm and the girl walked into my classroom.

"Mr. Capetz, I'm sorry to interrupt your class, but Susan can identify the student who broke our school door. Susan, do you see him in this room?"

"Yes, Miss Psalm! There he is! He's the boy with the blond hair and striped shirt," she blurted out.

She pointed her finger directly at me. I felt worse than having Mom yell at me with my hand in the cookie jar. All my classmates were looking at me, but what was worse was Mr. Cabot's stare. It melted me like ice! I wanted to crawl into a hole and hide from everyone.

"So, Tommy, it was you! I should have known because you're such a trouble maker. Get up out of your seat and come to my office!" Miss Psalm screamed.

I stood up to follow Miss Psalm to her office. She thanked the little girl for identifying me.

Susan smiled and said, "You're welcome, Miss Psalm. If I can ever help you again, please let me know." Then she smiled at me in a sarcastic way and walked back to her classroom. At that moment, I hated that little tattletale. But in some strange way, I was glad I was caught and didn't have to carry that broken handle on my conscience forever.

As we walked out of the room, I looked over at Bruce. His head was down, and he didn't even look up. I walked into Miss Psalm's office. She followed me and slammed the door.

"You had a chance to confess, Young Man, when I asked you to come to my office. But no, I had to come looking for you and dig you out like a rat out of a hole. Now tell me! What is the meaning of all this?"

"I don't know," I said without lifting my head.

"You look at me, Thomas, when I'm talking to you! Do you understand!" she shouted. "There was another boy with you. What was his name?"

I looked up at her with tears in my eyes and didn't respond.

"Well, Thomas? I'm waiting!" she said glaring at me. "You don't seem to understand, Young Man! You're in big trouble because you endangered the lives of your fellow students and damaged school property. Now, I'll ask you again! Who was with you?"

"Miss Psalm, I put the hockey stick between the door handles. I did it by myself. No one forced me to do it," I said with my voice cracking. I was really scared but didn't want to get Bruce in trouble.

Just then there was a knock on Miss Psalm's closed door. "I'm busy!" she shouted. "It will have to wait!" When the knocking persisted, she got up from behind her desk and stomped across the floor to open the door. She flung the door open, and Bruce was standing there. "What is it, Young Man?"

"I was with Tommy, Miss Psalm, and I'm just as guilty as he is because it was my idea," Bruce confessed in a soft voice.

"Well then, you'd better come in too!" she continued. "You boys committed a serious crime. Many children could have been seriously injured by your actions. There will be heavy consequences besides paying for the damage to the door."

As she continued, I felt a little better having Bruce beside me. He didn't have to turn himself in, but he was my buddy. We were going to weather this storm together.

"Are your parents home?" she asked.

"My mom is," I responded.

"No, my mom is working, "Bruce stated.

Miss Psalm called Mom and told her what we had done. She said she wanted me punished and separated from Bruce. She said Bruce and I were not a good influence on each other, and she was going to put us in different classrooms. She also said we would receive a bill for the damaged door. Then, she sent us back to our classrooms.

It was near the end of the day when we walked back into our class. Everyone looked at us as we quietly went to our seats. Mr. Capetz didn't say anything but just kept teaching. We opened our books and tried to listen to him, but our minds just wouldn't engage. Finally, the bell rang and school was over. As we got up to leave, Mr. Capetz said, "Could you two sit back down and wait until everyone leaves? I would like to have a little talk with you." We both went back to our seats and waited for everyone to leave.

When the room was empty, he said, "Come up here to my desk and bring a couple of chairs."

He pulled his chair out from behind his desk, and we sat in a little circle. "Now," he said, "I want to hear the whole story, and I want it straight! Do you understand?"

Bruce began, "We just wanted to have a little fun, Mr. Capetz. We didn't really mean any harm."

"Yeah, and when the kids were all pushing against the door, we couldn't have got that stick out even if we wanted to," I joined in.

He listened intently as we told him the whole story. We tried not to leave anything out. We trusted Mr. Capetz!

"Mr. Capetz, Miss Psalm is going to remove one of us from your room. She thinks we're a bad influence on each other," I said.

Mr. Capetz thought for a long time before saying anything. "You boys did a foolish thing. You didn't think about what could happen. Now, you're in trouble and I'm not going to punish you anymore. I'm sure Miss Psalm and your parents will do that. What I want to know is, how do you feel about what you have done?"

"We feel terrible!" Bruce said. "We never thought the door would break. We were just going to make them wait a little while and then let them out. Honest, Mr. Capetz!"

"Yeah, we're really sorry!" I threw in. "We never thought all this would happen! I'm going to shovel walks to earn the money to pay for the door because my parents can't afford another expense."

"Well, boys, I forgive you," said Mr. Capetz. "And even if it costs me my job, I'm not going to let Miss Psalm take either of you out of my class! I have begun to work with you, and no one is going to change that until it's over in June. Is that clear?"

"Yes, Mr. Capetz," we both said.

"We don't want to leave your room either!" I responded.

I don't know what Mr. Capetz said to Miss Psalm, but both of us stayed together the whole year. My parents grounded me for two weeks. I got three slaps with the razor strap and had to pay twenty-eight dollars for my half of the bill. Bruce and I learned a big lesson that year. More importantly, we found a friend neither of us will ever forget. Mr. Capetz left Miles Standish School after that year but kept in touch with us throughout our school years. I was sure glad the paths of our lives crossed because he was exactly what I needed at that time in my life. He was a real person, and I could relate to him.

Mr. Capetz spent time with us and talked to us. Mr. Capetz knew I loved sports, especially hockey, and found a book for me called Lightening on Ice. He said, "Tommy, I read this book about hockey and really liked it. Would you read it and give me your impression?"

I read the whole book in about three days. It was wonderful! We talked about the book together. That little incident got me reading for the first time in my life. It was the first book I had ever read from cover to cover! I'll always be grateful to Mr. Capetz for opening the wonderful world of books to me.

Mr. Capetz also used humor very effectively. One day he slapped me on the back of my head. It wasn't hard, just kind of a tap. I responded by saying, "What did you do that for?"

He said, "It's for all the things you've done and gotten away with." Then, he smiled and walked away. I smiled too because I knew he was right.

I think Bruce and I were Mr. Capetz' favorites. I couldn't imagine ever being a favorite of any teacher. He even came to some of our high school games when we got older. I often wondered if sticking up for us cost him his job at our school. I guess I will never know. But one thing I do know is, I'm a fifth grade teacher today and I pattern my style after good old Mr. Capetz. He'll never know what a huge influence he had on both of our lives.

The Principal

Miss Psalm, and I had a relationship. We got to know each other quite well. Unfortunately, I spent many hours in her office. One incident particularly caused her to be very upset with me. It was in the evening while she was conducting a P.T.A. meeting in our school gym. She was standing in front talking to all the parents. I climbed up onto the school roof by opening the large door and scaling it to reach the flat roof. The flat roof had little stones and tar on it. There were windows up there overlooking the gym. As Miss Psalm was speaking, she glanced up and saw me looking in the windows. I made a face at her and stuck out my tongue. This made her really upset, and she stopped speaking. She called in the janitor and pointed up at me. I knew I was in real trouble.

The janitor came flying out of the school and put a ladder up to the roof. I couldn't get to the door to get down. I could see I was going to get caught and began to panic! Just as the janitor reached the top of the roof, I jumped! I hit the ground with a crash and rolled. All my practice of jumping out of trees helped me out on this occasion, although I had never jumped from that height before. I got up and ran home with the janitor yelling at me to come back.

The next day Miss Psalm called me down to her office. She said, "Tommy, you humiliated and embarrassed me last night in front of all the parents. For this action you will be severely punished. I have never been so angry with a student as I am with you, Young Man! This will never happen again, and I will make sure of that! What's your telephone number?"

"It's Parker 1870."

"Mrs. Hall, this is Miss Psalm. It's about your son, Thomas, again."

She explained the whole story to my mom. When I got home from school, Mom was waiting for me. She was really upset! She began to cry and told me how disappointed she was. This always made me feel bad because I didn't like to see Mom cry. The next step was worse. She said, "You're going to have to face your father when he comes home from work." This made me very nervous because I knew what was coming. I went to my room and waited. Finally, I heard my father come in the door. I looked at him through the crack in my door and saw him give my mother a kiss. He did this every night when he entered the house. Then, I heard them talking in very low voices for about fifteen minutes. Next, I heard his footsteps coming to my bedroom. When he walked in, I could tell that he wasn't very happy!

"Son, your mother told me what you did at school last night!" he stated. "Do you have anything to say?"

"No, Dad."

"I don't know what I'm going to do with you! You're embarrassing Mom and me, always getting into trouble! Do you have an explanation?"

"No, Dad. It just happened," I responded.

"Well, you're going to be punished, Son." Even when he was mad at me, he still called me Son. I knew he still loved me even when I made him angry.

"First of all, you are grounded for two weeks. You come right home after school and go to your room. You cannot leave this house or even go into the yard. Do you understand?"

"Yes, Dad."

"Secondly, you will write a letter of apology to Miss Psalm and hand it to her saying you're sorry you embarrassed her. Is that clear?"

"Yes."

"Third, you can go down to the bathroom and bring up my razor strap."

Dad waited in my room as I walked to the bathroom and got his razor strap. I feared this but never resented it. I came back to my bedroom and saw him sitting on my bed. He had to spank me a lot, and I knew it was hard on him.

39

King of the Mountain

Recess was an interesting time for us on the playground at Standish. A lot of energy was released, like a popping cork from its bottle. But in this case, it was kids exploding from a classroom. No adults supervised the playground, so we were pretty much on our own. One day we played King of the Mountain, and Gail was the king. Gail was the toughest, meanest kid in the school. No one messed with her. She was a large girl and about as wide as she was tall. She kind of looked like a bulldog. She was very strong and struck fear into the heart of everyone foolish enough to cross her. Gail stood on top of a little hill, and no one could throw her off. Bodies flew everywhere as futile attempts were made to knock her off the hill.

Bruce and I stood at the bottom of the hill watching this incredible scene. No one came even close to knocking her off her feet. "Bruce," I said, "let's bring her down. No girl can be that tough."

"Are you crazy, Tommy?" Bruce said. "She will chew us up and eat us for lunch."

"I just can't stand seeing her stay on that hill, Bruce. I know that together we can knock her off! When she is distracted with some of the other kids, we'll charge and each drive our shoulders into her and the hill will be ours!" I said.

"Yeah, and when she comes back up the hill, we'll be dead meat!" whispered Bruce.

40

"I can't believe what I'm hearing! Bruce Wakefield, who fears nothing, is afraid of a girl!."

"Okay, Tommy, but I'm telling you this will not be as easy as you make it sound."

Bruce and I waited for just the right moment, and I yelled, "NOW!" We ran up the hill yelling as we went like a couple of uncontrollable hogs. Just as she turned, we drove both of our shoulders into her belly. She made a gasping sound and tumbled down the hill. Everyone was cheering as Bruce and I stood victorious on top of our little hill. Everyone, that is, except Gail! She charged up the hill glaring like a raging bull. She couldn't believe her eyes. Two little fifth graders just removed her from her prestigious spot. To the top of the hill she came, and no one got in her way. First, she grabbed Bruce and threw him half-way down the hill in mid-air. I wasn't so lucky. She looked at me and then doubled up her fist. So, I doubled up mine as the whole school circled around us to watch the massacre. I was scared but knew I couldn't back down. She hit me in the face with her right hand, and on her finger she wore a Lone Ranger Saddle Ring. The blow hurt and made two red marks on my face. I punched her in the stomach and hit her back in the face. She was furious! She charged into me like a linebacker, but I held my ground. I knew if I were knocked down it would be all over. She then hit me about five times in the face with such rapid blows that all I could do was cover up. As she came in for the kill, I sucker punched her. I was all doubled up and looked defeated when she moved in. I uncoiled and caught her with a right under her chin. She was surprised and staggered a bit. Finally, after exchanging blows back and forth, the bell rang. Everyone ran into the school.

Gail and I both ran in as well. I think we'd both had enough. I was cut up and bleeding, but I was a hero! I was the first person in our school who did not back down from Gail Armstrong. After that she left me alone. I guess I earned her respect.

When I came into the classroom, Mr. Capetz saw me and asked what had happened. "I slipped in the sand running in from recess and cut up my face a little," I said. He sensed that I didn't want to talk about it and didn't pursue it any further. I was glad!

Sibley Park

During fifth and sixth grade my horizons expanded. Sibley Park, which was one block from my new house, became my second home. Bruce also came to the park, but it was a mile walk for him. About the area of two city blocks, Sibley Park was located in a low area with large hills on each side. It had a large white building with a main floor and a basement. In the basement there was a large area with three ping-pong tables and several smaller rooms used for cooking classes, equipment storage, and wood working. The main floor had an office at one end and a large open area used for dances and special activities. The large grounds outside contained four tennis courts, three baseball diamonds, two horseshoe pits, a basketball court, a volleyball court, a wading pool, and a swing and sandbox area. You better believe we played all these sports too. It was like heaven for Bruce and me.

The city park system had a man and woman park instructor who worked each afternoon and evening during the school year. These park instructors taught classes, coached sports, and were available just to talk with kids. During the fall teams from all over the city came to play on the well lit football field. A large skating rink and a well lit hockey rink was flooded during the winter time. This is the place where Bruce and I continued our friendship. Our main interest was sports.

In the fall of our fifth grade year, we tried out for the Sibley Park football team. Most of the kids on the team were friends of ours at school. Our coaches were two fathers, Mr. Hastings and

Mr. Cooney. They were neat guys whose sons played on the team. Mr. Hastings was Mike's dad. He had been a great football player in high school. He was in his mid-forties, was well built and handsome, and had a good natured personality. Mr. Hastings played semi-pro baseball and was a great athlete. He really enjoyed working with us kids and laughed a lot. His easy going personality made it fun for us kids. Mr. Cooney was Terry's dad. Terry later became my best friend in high school. Mr. Cooney was a little more serious and used to tell us his philosophy all the time. He also was a high school baseball and football star. He was slender, well built, and athletic. Mr. Cooney would tell us how to win and talked to us about our attitudes and inner strength. They were both good men to have as our first coaches.

Bruce and I did very well in the tryouts. He played fullback and I played quarterback. We practiced under the lights every night after supper. Our coaches taught us how to block, tackle, pass, kick, and run. Bruce emerged as the top player on our team. He was hard to bring down because he was so shifty. He would give you a lame leg and then take off leaving you totally faked out. He was also a powerful runner. When met head on, Bruce would lift his knees so high it hurt to bring him down. It usually took two or three of us to tackle him. I had a good passing arm and called all the plays on offense. We both also played defense and enjoyed the contact part of the game. We loved tackling people. It was an exciting season playing under the lights. Many parents and friends came to watch us play. However, my parents seldom came, and Bruce's parents never came. It didn't matter though because we both loved to play football. We had a very good season and won most of our games. Mr. Hastings and Mr. Cooney taught us to enjoy football and, at the same time, built confidence in our athletic ability.

As the fall season ended and the trees became bare, we waited for that first snowfall. When it finally came like a quiet thief in the night, we woke up to a wonderful world with everything pure and sparkling white. After school we ran home, got our sleds, and all met on top of the big hills of Sibley Park. We used these hills in much the same way as otters sliding down a snowbank into an ice cold stream. Everything was the same except the cold stream.

"Hey, guys, there comes Bruce with his sled," I said as Bruce walked toward us pulling his sled behind him. His sled was blue with runners on the bottom. On the front of his sled, a horizontal piece of wood stuck out on each side and served as the steering handle. The wooden handle connected to the runners and would move from side to side allowing the driver of the sled to turn it to the right or to the left. The sled was about three and a half feet long. We laid on our stomachs while sliding down the hill. We got a running start, jumped on our sleds, and went down the hill with our legs bent upward at the knees. In this way we did not drag our legs and could get greater speed. We all had similar sleds.

"How long have you guys been here?" asked Bruce as he approached us.

"We just got here a little while ago," I said, "and have only taken a couple of runs."

"Let me take a couple of runs, so I can get warmed up," said Bruce as he ran toward the hill and jumped on his sled as smoothly as a bobsled runner in the Olympics. We all watched as he raced down the hill turning his sled from side to side making smooth 's' shape tracks in the snow. Then, we all jumped on our sleds and followed him down the hill. The temperature was about ten degrees above zero, and the cool crisp afternoon had already turned dark. However, the streetlights and the lights from the park gave us plenty of light. A powdery snowfall with light flakes fell nonchalantly from the sky. We were dressed in our winter gear which included boots, long underwear, jeans, a jacket, chopper mittens, and a stocking hat. We could stay outside for hours and never feel the cold.

At the bottom of the hill, Bruce called us all together. "Let's go to the top of the hill and form a train."

"How we gonna do that?" asked Waldo. Waldo was a new kid in the neighborhood and was just beginning to get to know everyone. Waldo lived a couple of blocks from the park too, but in the opposite direction from my house. He was short, wore glasses, and was not afraid to try anything.

"Well, Waldo," said Bruce.

"Call me Walt. I like that better," said Waldo.

"No, I'll call you Waldo because I like that better," Bruce replied. "We'll go to the top of the hill and start in the corner. Then, we'll all get on our sleds and hook our toes into the sled behind us. We'll begin by going down the sidewalk and then turn to the steeper part of the hill. Don't anyone let their feet slip out of the sled behind them, and we'll form a huge train going down the hill. I'll be the engine!" stated Bruce.

We went to the top of the hill and formed a train. The toes of our boots fit perfectly into the two openings of the sled behind us. It worked perfectly, just as Bruce had said. As Bruce and I were walking up the hill after our third run, I asked him, "Where did you come up with that idea, Bruce?"

"I don't know," he said. "Just thought it would be fun. That's all. Do you know what I want to do now, Tommy?"

"No. What?"

"Let's pick teams, slide down the hill, and try to knock each other off our sleds."

"Hey! That's another great idea!" I said. "You and I are on the same team. Okay?"

"I would have it no other way, Tommy. You know that!"

When we got to the top of the hill, Bruce explained the new game to everyone. We picked teams, and there were four on each team. If anyone got knocked off their sled, they were out. The team with the most guys left on their sleds won the game. During the first run Terry turned his sled into mine, grabbed my coat, and tried to drag me off my sled. At the same time, Bruce

45

turned his sled into Terry's. He pulled Terry off his sled and sent him rolling down the hill like a giant snowball.

"Thanks, Bruce!" I said. "I thought he had me."

"You did a nice piece of work just staying on your sled," he said. This was how we spent our November and December evenings until something more exciting came along. However, our pure love came in mid-winter. We could hardly wait for the rinks to be flooded so we could skate.

The first time we skated, Bruce and I went into the warming house to put on our skates. The warming house was a portable building the city put up each winter at the park. It was a rectangular wooden building with a front and a back door. Inside the building sat rows of benches for us to sit on to change into our skates. A potbelly stove heated with coal stood in the middle of the building. It had a iron railing around it and a smokestack running through the roof. The building wasn't much to look at, but it kept us warm and was our home for the winter.

Bruce had new skates that he had gotten for Christmas, and I had a pair of used soft toe hockey skates which were two sizes too big for me. We laced up our skates and went outside. Bruce took off like a jet across the hard white ice. I, however, really struggled. My feet went every which way. I was like a duck on ice. Bruce would skate by and spin me around. I'd fall flat on my face. Once again, I was impressed at his natural athletic ability. Without ever taking a skating lesson, Bruce was zooming all over the rink. It always took me a lot longer. I had to work hard to learn the same skill he learned right away. That determination and hard work did pay off as we got older. Meanwhile, I never gave up. Pretty soon my ankles strengthened, and I began to skate all over the ice too.

We mostly enjoyed skating on the big main rink at first. We loved to play games such as Pom Pom Pull-a-Way and Prisoner's Base. Bruce was always the last one to be caught because he could skate so well. There could be twenty of us trying to catch him. He would skate around the bench on the rink a couple of times to get up speed. Then, he would streak across the ice with all of us chasing him. He would zig zag, cut, turn, jump, and stop quickly to get away from people. He was so smooth that it was like watching poetry in motion. The only way we could catch him was by tiring him out. I remember chasing him and skating as fast as my legs could move when he stopped suddenly. I had not mastered the art of stopping yet and landed head first in a big snowdrift. We had a big laugh about that as he pulled me out of the snowdrift that almost completely swallowed me up. During that year we skated together almost every day.

I talked my dad into taking me to the Skate Exchange to get a pair of skates that actually fit me properly. By the end of the year, I was skating almost as well as Bruce. He was still a little faster and stronger on his skates, but not that much better.

Cold Reality at Sibley

One Saturday I woke up at eight in the morning. Mom fixed us a nice breakfast of bacon, eggs and toast. After breakfast I went into the bathroom and cleaned up. As I brushed my teeth, I looked at them in the mirror. I rinsed my mouth with cold water and lifted my lip to examine my teeth again. I was proud of them because they were so white and straight. Then, I went down the basement and dug through all the hockey equipment. My brothers and I piled all our equipment together in the basement at the end of a day. In order to go skating the next day, we always had to rummage through all the equipment to find our own stuff. This was not an easy task with five brothers.

Our basement was not finished off. It had a large furnace with big pipes going in every direction. The furnace had been converted from burning coal to using natural gas. A narrow stairway led to the basement. The floor was a concrete slab, and the walls were cement blocks. The ceiling was the exposed wooden floor joists and flooring above. Mom had an old washer with a wringer down there. There was also a washtub with two water spouts. At one end of the basement was Dad's workshop, which was filled with old tools. This workshop had once been a room for storing coal. We called it the coal bin. At the other end of the basement was a fruit cellar. Mom used this room to store canned and bottled food she prepared from our summer garden. The basement was usually dark and messy and only cleaned about once a year. There were always spider webs around.

I sat down on the cold floor and put on my long underwear.

48

Next, I put on a pair of wool socks and tucked my underwear in them so my legs would not be exposed to the cold. I put my shin pads around my legs. They fit nicely around my legs and had a leather piece connected to a wider part that covered my knee. They would bend there giving my legs mobility. I strapped the shin pads to my legs with leather straps connected to the pads. If I did not wear these pads, my legs would get all bruised up from sticks and flying pucks. I then put on my supporter and cup. This protected my genital area from being injured. I once made the mistake of going to the park to play hockey without wearing this vital little piece of equipment. I was hit by a hard frozen rubber puck in that area of my anatomy and went down on the ice with a mighty crash. I could not stand up. Two of my friends helped me into the warming house. With an arm draped over each of their shoulders, they dragged me across the ice and up the stairs and plopped me down on the bench. I could not skate even one stride or take a step. I sat in the warming house and moaned for two solid hours. Eventually, the pain subsided. Needless to say, I learned very quickly never to be without that protective device again. Next, I pulled my pants over my pads and cup and pulled them up. I put on my sweatshirt, zipped up my blue tanker jacket, and put on my stocking hat. I found my hockey stick and put my skates on it. Finally, I put on my chopper mittens and headed upstairs. Mom came flying outside as she heard the back door slam. As I was walking down the back stairs, I heard her yell, "Get back into this house, Young Man!"

I turned around and went back inside. "What's the problem?" I asked in a bewildered voice.

"It's too cold! That's what's the matter," she stated in a very determined voice.

"How cold is it, Mom?" I responded casually.

"It's eighteen below zero!" she stated. "And, you will freeze to death!"

"Awe, Mom, that's not so cold," I said. "And besides, if I get cold then I'll just go into the warming house and warm up."

"I forbid you to go skating today, Tommy! Is that clear?"

"Mom, Bruce is down there waiting for me! We go skating every Saturday morning no matter what. I can't let him down. Sorry, Mom, but I have to go skating," I said and walked out the door. I heard her say as I left, "I just don't know what I'm going to do with that boy!"

When I got to the top of Sibley Hill just a short block from my house, I pulled my stocking cap over my ears. I usually didn't need to do this, but today my ears felt really cold. I looked down the hill and saw the huge skating rink with a fresh sheet of ice shining in the sun. The hockey rink was next to the main rink and empty. I saw the portable wooden warming house next to the main building and noticed a billow of smoke coming out of the chimney stack. I jumped over the iron rail fence where I once left part of my tongue. Don't ever stick your warm tongue on a cold iron rail fence in Minnesota. It simply won't come off. I learned that lesson, like most other lessons in my life, the hard way! I ran down the hill and walked up to the warming house. The place was deserted. I flung open the door and saw Bruce sitting by the potbelly stove with his skates on and feet stretched over the iron rail that surrounded the stove.

"Tommy, I thought you'd never get here!" he said casually.

"You knew I'd be here!" I said. "I'll never pass up a Saturday to play hockey no matter how cold it gets," I said. Bruce and I were known as rink rats because we skated as often as we could during the ice season.

"Hurry and put on your skates," he said. "We have the rink to ourselves today."

Bruce slid over on the bench and helped me tighten my skates. He knew I liked my skates tight. I pulled two laces tight, and he held the laces down with his thumb while I went on to the next two laces. Bruce didn't seem to need tight skates and just tied his skates by himself. I think his ankles were so strong that it just didn't matter to him. On the other hand, I always needed my skates really tight. We walked down the wooden stairway and jumped onto the ice. The ice was hard and cold. It was so cold there were splits or cracks in the ice. Believe it or not, the temperature can even be too cold for good ice. About ten degrees above zero is the perfect temperature to skate in. Bruce and I could skate all day at that temperature and even work up a sweat.

We skated for about an hour and played hockey together. We passed the puck back and forth and stick handled all over the rink. "Let's go in and warm up for a while, Bruce," I said.

"Okay, sounds good to me," he responded. "I still can't believe no one is down here," he said.

"Yeah," I said, "I thought Terry would be down here for sure. He never misses a chance to skate."

We went inside to warm up and took off our skates and socks. Our toes were bright red. We rubbed them back and forth in our hands to get the circulation going again. Then, we leaned back on the bench and let them thaw while we dangled them over the iron railing by the potbelly stove. We moaned in pain as they slowly thawed out. The stove was so hot that its sides were glowing red.

"I wonder what would happen if I rubbed the back end of my hockey stick against the stove," Bruce said as he picked up his stick. He pressed his stick against the stove and held it there for a minute or two. Suddenly, it burst into flames.

"Cool," I said as I reached for my stick. We experimented lighting our sticks on fire and putting them out again. Finally, our feet thawed out. It's funny how once your feet freeze and then thaw out, it then seems like you can go out again and skate forever. They are all right as long as they're bright red. However, if they turn white, you're in big trouble. This also happened to us on a couple of occasions when we stayed out a little too long on a below zero evening.

"Let's go out and skate some more," Bruce said as he got up to go out on the rink.

"Hey, wait a second, Bruce. Aren't you forgetting something?" I said.

"I swear! I don't know what you'll do when you don't have me to help you tighten you skates," he said as he came back and helped me lace up my skates.

Once we were back out on the ice, we flew all over the rink. We felt as free as birds gliding through the air as we sailed over the hard ice.

"I've got an idea, Tommy. Let's see who can keep the puck away from the other the longest." He pulled a puck out of his pocket and threw it on the hard ice. "You start first," he said. "I'll count to ten and then chase you."

I took off and he came flying after me. I cut around but couldn't shake him off of me. Finally, with a neat sweep check, he took the puck from me and skated in the opposite direction. I stopped sharply sending ice chips flying into the air. Bruce cut, twisted, and turned to keep himself between me and the puck. I marveled at his skill but in my determination managed to take the puck from him. This exchange went on for about an hour. We were both so tired that we felt like we would drop. Finally, Bruce got the puck and said, "I'm never going to give it up this time, Tommy!"

"We'll see about that!" I said as I streaked after him. He really turned on the afterburners, but there was no way I would not catch him. I reached inside and began pumping my legs as fast as I could. Suddenly, bam!! I was flat on my face sprawled out on the ice. My skate had caught in a crack on the ice, and I fell on my hockey stick. My mouth was open so my two front teeth were pushed into my mouth. Because it was so cold, my brittle teeth just snapped without any blood. As I opened my mouth, the cold air hit an exposed nerve and sent a shrieking pain to my brain. I quickly covered my mouth with my mitten. Bruce saw me laying on the ice and came flying back. He stopped sharply right in front of me and bent down and said, "Are you all right, Tommy?"

I couldn't speak but just motioned him to take me into the warming house. We skated into the warming house and took off our skates. "Let's go see the park instructor, Tommy," Bruce said. He took me by the arm and led me into the main building. Roger Larson was working that day. He was a nice guy and knew Bruce and me very well. He saw me holding my mouth and said, "What's wrong, Tommy?"

I opened my mouth and spit my two front teeth on his desk and smiled. He made an awful face and said, "Oh no, Tommy! You'd better go home immediately and show your parents. Bruce and I got our things and headed for home. We didn't say a thing to each other when we reached my house. He just put his arm around my shoulder, and I walked into my house. Mom saw me holding my mouth and turned white. "What did you do, Tommy?" she shouted. I opened my mouth and she screamed. "Tommy, those were your permanent teeth. I told you not to go skating. You just won't listen to me. What am I going to do with you? And you had such beautiful teeth. Tommy, how are we going to pay the dentist bill?" She went on and on.

I walked into the bathroom and looked into the mirror. It was the same mirror I had just looked into that morning admiring my beautiful teeth. I smiled and couldn't believe my eyes. My teeth were chipped off! I looked like a witch. I wanted to die. When I walked out into the living room, Mom was still yelling. I was shocked, hurt, and needed comfort. When I received none, I ran down to the basement. I went into a dark corner and sobbed and sobbed. I stayed there all night. I refused to come up to eat or even go to bed. Mom knew I was hurt. She let me stay in the basement. The next morning she came down and woke me. She had settled down by then.

"Tommy, I made a dentist appointment," she said. "I'm sorry I was so angry last night."

I jumped into her arms. "Mom, I look like a witch," I said. "I will have to stay like this my whole life. I can't get new teeth."

"Now, Son," she said. "The dentist can take care of you. Everything will be all right. I promise!"

The dentist said he could not cap my teeth because they were still growing. I spent a couple of weeks going around with chipped teeth. I looked so awful that I hardly ever opened my mouth. Then, one night I woke up and felt a big red thing hanging from my tooth. I didn't know what to do, so I bit it. It was a nerve! I screamed because the pain was so excruciating. I forced myself back to sleep. The next morning the nerve went back into my tooth. I told Mom and she made an emergency appointment for me. The dentist examined me and found my teeth had abscessed. That meant they were filled with poison! The dentist pulled the remaining parts of my chipped teeth out, and at age eleven I was fitted with false teeth. I thought I would never get used to a plate on the roof of my mouth, but eventually I did. At least I had teeth again and looked a little better.

The Yo-Yo Man

Bruce and I met on the playground just before school began. "Hi, Bruce," I said as I approached him on the school playground.

"Hey, what's happening, Tommy?" he said.

"Not much. I hope we get some excitement in school today."

"Yeah! Same here. Life's been a little too routine for me lately."

The school bell rang as we walked toward the building together. We hung up our jackets in the cloakroom and sat down at our desks. Our teacher stood up and announced, "Today we have a surprise for you! We are having a school assembly. A man is going to demonstrate how to work the yo-yo."

Bruce looked over at me and rolled his eyes. "This ought to be great," he said sarcastically.

"Oh, well," I sighed. "At least we get out of a little school work."

We walked down to the gym where all the classes were being seated on the floor. Our principal, Miss Psalm, gave the introduction, "A man is here from the Duncan Yo-Yo Company. He's going to demonstrate how to use a new toy called the yo-yo. Actually, it's not very new because it has been around for centuries. Please give a nice warm welcome to the 'Yo-Yo Man.'" Everyone gave a courtesy clap.

A short man walked onto the stage. He was dark complected and wore a pullover sweater which said Duncan Yo-Yo on the front of it. He told us a little history about the yo-yo. "My people invented the yo-yo. I'm from the Philippine Islands. They are a small group of islands located in the South Pacific Ocean. The first yo-yos were used by my people as a weapon to hunt and kill small animals. My ancestors would climb trees and when a small animal passed by, such as a rabbit, they would throw their yo-yos down from the tree. If they hit the animal, they had dinner that evening. If they missed, they simply wound their yo-yos up and tried again. As time progressed our weapons became more sophisticated. The yo-yo was replaced by better weapons. The yo-yo then became a popular toy among the children."

Bruce and I were sitting together and listening intently because the guy was a pretty good speaker. Then, he pulled a yo-yo from his pocket.

"This, boys and girls, is the greatest toy ever invented," he said as he put the string around his middle finger and threw the yo-yo down really hard so it spun around very fast. He let it sit there for about twenty seconds then, with a small jerk of his hand, snapped it up again.

"Wow! Bruce, did you see that?" I exclaimed.

"Yeah! That was really cool!" he replied.

The Yo-Yo Man held us all spellbound for about half an hour. He made that yo-yo do everything but talk. Bruce and I hardly took our eyes off him as he did trick after trick. He had names for all his tricks. He did Stall, Walk the Dog, Creeper, Around the Corner, Over the Falls, Rock the Baby in the Cradle, Around the World, Loop the Loop, and many others. He even threw the yo-yo between his legs, and it landed inside his pocket. Needless to say, he impressed us all and especially Bruce and me! When he finished, we broke into a thunderous roar. He walked off the stage, but we continued to clap and shout, "More! More!"

The Yo-Yo Man walked back onto the stage and said, "Thank you for that nice response!" Then, he proceeded to do some almost unbelievable things with the yo-yo. He did tricks called Man on the Flying Trapeze and Brain Twister, and then he threw the yo-yo high into the air and it landed in his shirt pocket. Bruce and I had never seen anything quite like this before. When he finished, Miss Psalm got up and quieted us all down. Our class lined up to go back to our room. "Bruce, I've got to go talk to that guy!" I said. I left our line and headed toward the front of the gym to see the Yo-Yo Man. Bruce was right behind me. When I reached him, his back was toward me. I tapped him on the shoulder and said, "Sir, you are great! I've never seen anything quite like that before."

"Yeah," said Bruce. "How did you ever learn to do all those tricks?"

"Is that a trick yo-yo or can anyone learn to do those tricks?" I threw in.

"Well, boys," he said, "I'm glad you liked the show. No, this isn't a trick yo-yo. It's just a simple wooden Duncan yo-yo. You can buy them at any drug store for thirty-five cents. Here is a list of the basic tricks," he said as he handed me a little pamphlet.

"Could I have another one for my friend?" I asked.

"Sure," he said. "I'll give you each a couple of extra strings in case you break yours," he added. "In a couple of weeks, I'll be back for a yo-yo contest. Get yourselves a yo-yo and have some fun with it."

"Gee, thanks, Mister!" I said. I gave the extra pamphlet to Bruce and said, "We gotta get ourselves a yo-yo, Bruce!"

Bruce got thirty-five cents from his mom, and I raked the neighbor's leaves for my thirty-five cents. We went down to Scott's Drug Store and bought our very own yo-yos. Mine was red with a white stripe down the middle, and Bruce's was blue with a white stripe down the middle. We unwrapped the packages, put the string on our middle finger, and tried to work our new yo-yos. Not only could we not work them, but we couldn't even wind them up. As hard as we tried, we could not get them to work.

"That guy tricked us," I said in frustration. "These yo-yos don't even work!"

"Yeah, he just wanted us to buy these stupid yo-yos. That's all!" said Bruce.

"Hey, he's coming back to our school to do a contest. Let's find him and give him a piece of our mind," I stated.

On Thursday after school as Bruce and I walked out of the building, we spotted the Yo-Yo Man on the playground. There were several kids around him. We walked over to him and listened as he explained the rules of the contest. "You each get two chances for each trick. If you miss the trick, then you're out. You will all have to do the eight basic tricks. From those who can do them all, we decide the winner with Loop the Loops." Then, he demonstrated how to do Loop the Loop. He threw the yo-yo out in front of him and snapped his wrist. The yo-yo swung inside his arm and outside again so fast that we could hardly see it. He did ten loops in a couple of seconds.

About ten kids lined up for the contest. When it was their turn, they each stepped out and tried the trick. If they were successful, they stepped back in line. If not, they tried again. If they missed the second time, they were out. No one could do all the basic tricks. The winner was a fifth grade girl, and she received a nice pullover sweater.

After the contest Bruce and I walked up to the Yo-Yo Man. "We think you tricked us," Bruce said. "Tom and I bought Duncan yo-yos at the drug store, and we can't even wind them up!"

"Do you have your yo-yos, boys?" he said.

"I do!" I said. I pulled it from my pocket and handed it to him.

He put the string on his finger and snapped it up to his hand. He then threw it down sideways and let it spin. "That trick is called the butterfly. It adjusts the string for you. If you want to tighten the string, you throw it to your right. If you want to loosen the string, you just throw it to your left." He took my yo-yo and did about fifteen fabulous tricks. Bruce and I just stood and watched in amazement. He then handed the yo-yo back to me. "There's nothing wrong with your yo-yo. As a matter of fact, it has a rather nice balance," he said. "It's is my fault, though, that you feel that way. I should have given you more instructions. First, you need to understand the principle of how a yo-yo works. The strings are made in the factory. They are strong and wound around to form a loop on the bottom. That loop slips over the yo-yo. Let me show you how it works." He loosened his yo-yo and took off the string. "Do you see this string?" he said. "You just slip it over the yo-yo and pull it tight. A yo-yo is just two round pieces of wood connected together by a smooth wooden dowel. When the string is loose, the yo-yo will freely spin around the string. When the string is tighter, it will not spin as freely. Some tricks need a loose string. For example, Rock the Baby is a trick that needs a loose string." He threw his yo-yo down, made a cradle with the string, and rocked the yo-yo back and forth through the cradle. He continued, "Other tricks need a tighter string." He threw the yo-yo at an angle so it spun on its side, and then he snapped it back to his hand again. "That trick is called the Butterfly," he said again. "It's a quick way to adjust your string for each trick you do." Then, he did ten quick loops. "There's nothing wrong with your yo-yo," he said. "Just learn to adjust your string, and you will be fine. Oh, by the way, I'll be at Sibley Park in a couple weeks for another contest. Hope to see you boys there!"

"Well, I'll be darned!" I said to Bruce as we walked toward my house. "All we had to do was tighten our strings."

"I knew that!"

"Sure you did! You were the one who thought we'd been had by the Yo-Yo Man. You know, Bruce, I really like that guy!"

"Yeah, he is kind of nice. Do you think we can learn to do those tricks, Tommy?"

"I don't know about you, but he had to learn them some way so I'm sure going to try. How about you, Bruce?"

"Yeah, let's practice together until we can do all those basic tricks. You know something, Tommy? I'm going to win one of those contests."

"So am I, Bruce! So am I!"

Bruce and I practiced every night. First, we learned to throw our yo-yos. We could throw them down and out. Next, we learned how to make our yo-yos stall. Then, we learned the butterfly trick so we could adjust our strings. It took a couple of weeks, but we finally learned all the basic tricks. We practiced every night for two or three hours straight.

"Let's enter that contest down at Sibley tomorrow night, Tommy," Bruce said as we were practicing over at his house.

"Do you think we are ready?" I asked.

"We're as good as the kids we saw at school," he said. "Besides that, what do we have to lose?"

"Okay, let's give it a shot!"

"Fine! I'll pick you up after supper, and we'll go down to Sibley together."

The next evening Bruce came over, and we rode our bikes down to the park. The Yo-Yo Man was there getting things ready for the contest. When he saw us he said, "How are your broken yo-yos working?" We just smiled.

There were about twenty kids lined up in the basement of the park building for the contest. Lots of people watched. Bruce and I stood next to each other. "Good luck!" he said.

"Yeah, you too!"

Bruce and I made it successfully through five tricks. Only six people were left. The next trick was Around the Corner.

"I don't know about this trick, Bruce," I said.

"Hey, I know it's hard but we've both done it. So, don't sweat it!"

"Okay!"

The first two boys missed this trick. The Yo-Yo Man came to me. I threw my yo-yo down to clear the string. I was now ready to attempt the trick. I threw the yo-yo down and wrapped it around my arm. It jerked up too fast and lost its spin. I looked at Bruce and knew he was pulling for me.

"You have one more chance," said the Yo-Yo Man.

I tried it again and failed. I stepped out and hung my head. Then, I looked up and said, "Come on, Bruce. I know you can do it!"

Bruce threw his yo-yo down into a perfect stall. He wrapped the string around his arm and gave it a little jerk. The yo-yo came back to his hand perfectly. Everyone clapped. Bruce did all the basic tricks. Two boys and one girl did all the tricks, so the winner was decided by the person who could do the most Loop the Loops. Bruce did fifty-six loops and won the contest. He was given a sweater, a new yo-yo, and five strings. He came over to me after the contest, and we hugged each other.

"Hey, that was great, Man!"

"Yeah, can you believe it? Just three weeks ago we were both ready to throw our yo-yos away."

Bruce and I continued to practice. We actually got pretty good! Whenever we heard about a contest, we entered it. We were pretty even. Usually, he or I would win. Our yo-yos went with us everywhere. Bruce would buck me on the front handlebars of his bike while I did loops as we rode down the street. We always pulled for each other and never felt bad when the other person won. People all over the city knew about us and our yo-yos. We heard about a city contest down at Loring Park. This was a park near downtown Minneapolis. Kids from all over the city entered this contest. The winner would be the best yo-yoer in the whole city. The prize was a three-speed English bicycle. I wanted to win that contest more than anything in the world. I knew I could do all the basic tricks, and the winner would be decided by who could do the most loops. So, I practiced doing Loop the Loop every day. I realized the string needed to be real tight because after each loop the yo-yo would turn a half a turn. That meant the string got looser and looser until it was impossible to do any loops. As I practiced, I discovered it was possible to make the string cross over so it would begin to tighten again. I kept working on this until I had it down. When the string crossed over, I could do another one hundred loops. My record was four hundred. Bruce didn't practice as hard as I did.

Finally, the day for the big contest came. My dad drove us down to Loring Park. I was pumped up because of the contest and the fact that my dad would be watching me. He was very busy with our large family and was never able to watch any of my sporting events. When we got there, the place was crowded. There was a small lake surrounded by beautiful trees. The green grass, flowers, and trees made it one of the loveliest parks in the city of Minneapolis. There was a large pavilion where everyone was gathered. The Yo-Yo Man lined us all up in a straight line. There must have been fifty kids in this contest. I had seen many of these kids before because of all the contests I'd entered. My toughest competition was Bruce and Tom Reynolds. I had beaten Tom in a couple of contest before, but I knew that he was very good. It took about an hour to get through the basics. Bruce had missed on Rock the Baby in the Cradle. I felt bad because he usually could do this trick in his sleep. When we got to the finals, there were six of us left. I was the second one to do loops. I tightened my string as much as I could. I began pumping out the loops. I had done two hundred loops when the string began to get very loose. I kept spinning around to keep the yo-yo spinning. I got up to two hundred and fifty. I was trying to make the string cross over and tighten again. I spun around and hit the Yo-Yo Man who was holding a bag of prizes. My string wrapped around his bag. I was stopped at two hundred and fifty-five.

"That was no fair!" I protested. "You were in my way, and I could have done more loops!"

"No! You were at the end of your loops," said the Yo-Yo Man.

Tom Reynolds was the last person left in the contest. He tightened his string. He began very strongly. He did one hundred pretty easily. When he got to two hundred he was beginning to struggle. When he got to two forty, I began to pray that he would miss. He did two hundred and sixty loops. I was furious! I stomped up to that Yo-Yo Man and demanded another turn. I pleaded with him. I told him I was trying to make the string cross over so I could do another hundred loops. Nothing I said seemed to help. I continued to plead my case until the Yo-yo Man got really upset and screamed at me to sit down. I walked away sulking. Tom Reynolds won the bicycle, and I won a trophy for second place.

After the contest, I walked over to where my dad and Bruce were sitting under a tree. I thought my dad would be proud of me for getting second place in the contest. When I neared him he said, "I want to talk to you, Son! I am so disappointed in your behavior!"

"Dad, I should have won that contest! You saw him! He got in my way. I wanted that bike more than anything in the world!"

"Stop it, Tommy! There is something more important than winning a bicycle. It's who you are. And right now I am ashamed to call you my son. You embarrassed me! You acted like a spoiled child who didn't get his way. If you are ever going to be in a contest or sporting event again, I never want to see that behavior again! No matter whether you are right or wrong, the referee or judge has the last word. Your character is more important than winning or losing. You must learn to take losing like a man. That man was the judge. He made his decision. He was impartial. You should have respected his decision and abided by it. Do you understand?"

"Yes, Dad. I'm sorry. I don't want to disappoint you. Please forgive me. I promise you, it will never happen again!" And, I meant that too!

Pantsed

I t was a breathtaking Saturday afternoon. Light fluffy clouds were scattered sparsely throughout the soft blue sky. The grass was turning green, and the leaves were beginning to sprout in the trees. A gentle breeze blew in my face bringing a cool refreshment that made me feel good all over. I had just finished a tasty lunch Mom fixed and felt fully satisfied and refreshed. I was sitting on the back steps of my house when Bruce came over.

"Hey, Tommy! What's happening?"

"Nothing much," I said. "I just think it's a perfect day. That's all. Where you going?"

"Actually, I was coming to see you," he said. "Do you want to go to the park and see if there's any action down there?"

"Sounds great." I got up from the steps and began walking with him to the park. When we got there, the place was deserted. "There's no one around, Bruce. What do you want to do?" I asked.

"Have you got your knife?"

"Sure. It's in my pocket." I always carried a little pocket jack-knife. It had two blades, a large and a small one. We used the knife to play two games. One was called Knife and the other was called Stretch. In the game of Knife, the object was to throw the knife from different body positions and make it stick in the grass. You had to be able to place two fingers under it in order for the turn to count. We threw the knife with the palm of our hands to begin the game. The knife was then thrown from the back of our hands and our wrists, elbows, shoulders, forehead, nose, chin, and over our head. The final two tricks were called Over the Fence and Spin the Beer Bottle. In Over the Fence, we stuck the knife lightly into the ground, placed our hand in a vertical position, and flipped the knife over it so it stuck in the ground. In Spin the Beer Bottle, we placed the knife on the palm of our hand, flipped it a little, and then hit the handle causing it to turn many times in the air before sticking in the ground. It was difficult to do. We got two chances for each trick. If we missed, we had to begin all over again. The winner would get a small stick or branch from a tree. He stuck this in the ground and pounded it down with the back of the knife handle. The winner got three blows to drive the stick into the ground. The loser had to pull the stick out with his teeth, which was difficult when the stick was pounded into the ground. Bruce and I were pretty good at this game. We played for hours under the shade of an elm tree. On this particular day, however, I sensed that Bruce just wanted to talk.

"How do you feel about going to junior high next year, Tommy?" he asked as he threw the knife into the ground.

"Kind of scared, I guess," I responded. "We'll be the smallest kids in the school again, and some of those teenagers are pretty tough!"

"I'm not too worried about that," he said. "What bothers me is all the changes that will be happening. There will be kids from three different elementary schools going to Folwell Junior High. I wonder how we'll get along and mix together. I'll miss good old Standish School."

"Yeah! I will too. Who was your favorite teacher?"

"You don't have to ask that question! It was Capetz by far!"

"Yeah, he was my favorite teacher too! I wonder how he's doing at his new school?" I said.

"Do you like your new neighborhood, Tommy?" Bruce asked.

"It's okay. I miss the old neighborhood though. But our house is bigger, and now we can all fit. I also like being close to the park."

"I miss your family, Tommy," said Bruce with a far away look in his eyes. "Your mom really treated me nice. I hope you know how special she is?" he said.

"How is your dad doing?" I asked. "You know, for as many

times as I spent at your house, I don't feel I really know him."

"I don't know him either! He's gone a lot you know. He works at night clubs and travels a lot now. I don't think my mom and dad are too happy together. When I see your parents, Tommy, the way they treat each other and love all you guys, I'm so jealous! You don't have a lot of money, but you have a neat family. I just miss being in your home. Do you believe in God?"

"Wow! Where did that come from?" I asked.

"I don't know. I'm just curious. You go to church all the time, and your mom prays and reads the Bible. I just never asked you how you felt about it, that's all."

"Sure, I believe in God. Not like my mother though. She sees Him everywhere. She reads the Bible every night to my brothers and me. Then we pray and go to bed. I feel so good after she does that. It's like God is watching out for our family."

"The only time I ever go to church is with your family. I just don't know if there really is a God, Tommy. But when I see your family operating the way they do, I really begin to wonder."

"Bruce, I'll always believe in God! I just hope someday my faith will be as strong as my mother's. You're right, Bruce, she is an incredible lady."

"Hey! Do you want to play a game of Stretch?" said Bruce.

"Okay."

Stretch was a game with the knife too. We both stood facing each other with our feet together. One person would throw the knife into the ground, but it must turn once in the air. We used the little blade because it's better balanced. If it stuck in the ground, the other person stretched his foot to the knife and pulled it out of the ground. The knife couldn't be thrown more than two knife lengths at a time. Your legs got so stretched out it was almost like doing the splits. The first person to fall lost. We were at the park for a long time, and it was beginning to get dark. We looked up and saw Jimmy Nearinhousen coming down the park steps. He hadn't seen us yet.

"Hey! Let's have some fun with Nearinhousen," said Bruce as he pulled me behind some bushes.

Jimmy was a year younger than us. He was small and had red hair and freckles. He got spooked easily and was fun to tease.

"When he comes by we'll jump out and scare the crap out of him," Bruce said with a gleam in his eyes. Bruce had a tender side to him, but he also had a reckless side. "Then, let's pants him."

"I don't know, Bruce," I said.

"We won't hurt him. We'll just take off his pants and throw them up in this tree. Come on, Hall. Let's have a little fun!"

"Okay," I said reluctantly.

Jimmy came walking down the sidewalk whistling and happy as a lark. When he walked by the bushes, we jumped out and yelled! He jumped three feet in the air and turned white. "What are you guys doing?" he said as Bruce grabbed him around the chest pinning his arms to his side.

"Now, Tommy! Take off his pants."

Jimmy began kicking, screaming and swearing at us. Bruce held him tightly while I pulled off his pants. I handed them to Bruce, and he threw them up into the elm tree.

"How am I going to get my pants down, you guys?" pleaded Jimmy.

"Oh, I guess you're just going to have to climb the tree," said Bruce. We left him staring at his pants on a high branch in the tree. He looked pretty helpless standing there in his underwear.

We walked back through the park and up the hill heading for my house. I was feeling pretty guilty, but it didn't seem to bother Bruce at all. The sun had set and it was getting dark. As we walked down Fortieth Street, a black forty-nine Ford drove past us. The driver was looking at us closely as he drove by.

"Quick, Tommy, duck into the alley!" We ran into the alley and hid behind a garage. The car stopped at the end of the block, and we could see the driver with his arm over the seat looking at us.

"Who do you think it is?" asked Bruce.

"Maybe Nearinhousen called his dad and he came looking for us," I said.

"No way!" said Bruce. "He hasn't even had time to get his pants down from the tree yet. I have no idea who it is, but he sure is looking at us."

Then, Bruce walked out onto the sidewalk and said, "Come on, Tommy. We don't have anything to be afraid of."

Just then, the driver put his car in reverse and squealed his tires as he pealed backwards towards us.

"Run, Tommy!" Bruce yelled. Bruce ran down the street. I ran down the alley. The car stopped in front of the alley, and the driver jumped out and began chasing me. He was really fast and was gaining on me. My heart was pounding! I had no idea who this was. I thought I was being paid back for being so mean to Jimmy. I heard his footsteps close behind me. I had one advantage, though, because this was my turf. I felt his hand grab for me and miss. I dove down between two garages. A low fence connected the garages, so I wiggled under the fence just before the man could grab me. I felt like a rabbit escaping from a wolf. The man tried to follow me but got stuck under the fence. I heard him grunting and swearing as I ran over to Standish School and hid in the bushes by the building. The black Ford circled around the neighborhood for about a half hour. Finally, when it all seemed clear, I jumped out of the bushes and ran home. If I had been timed, I'm sure I would have set a world record for speed. Mom saw me fly through the door.

"What's wrong, Tommy?" she asked.

"Not a thing, Mom," I lied. "I just wanted to see how fast I could run home from the park. That's all!"

I never found out who the man was that chased me. I felt bad about what we had done to Jimmy. When I saw him in school, I apologized to him. He wasn't too quick to forgive me. Eventually though, he got over it, and we were friends again.

Mittens

During the winter when snow and ice became packed on the streets making them very slippery, Bruce and I hopped cars. It was mostly teenagers who attempted this dangerous and foolish feat, but Bruce and I got involved at the age of twelve. We learned this activity by watching teenagers at the top of Sibley Park hill. Cars always slowed down for this steep hill. As the cars slowed down, teenage boys would sneak up behind them, grab the steel bumper, and slide down the street. They slid on their boots in a crouched position as they hung onto the car's bumper.

Bruce and I were walking down to the park when we saw four teenage boys hiding behind a parked car. A car passed us going down the street heading toward Sibley Park. When the car passed the parked car, it slowed down for the hill. The four boys ran out and grabbed the bumper. We watched as they slid down the hill and out of sight.

"What do you think, Bruce?" I said.

"It looks like fun!"

"Do you think we could do that?" I questioned.

"We won't know unless we give it a try," he said. "Let's hide behind that same car. When another car comes by, we'll go for it!"

"Yeah, but when we do, we'll have to stay low so the driver won't see us out of his rear-view mirror," I said. So, we hid behind the parked car.

"Here comes a car, Hallsey," said Bruce excitedly. "Stay low and when I say 'Now' go for the bumper." The car passed us and slowed down for the hill. "Now," Bruce yelled! We both took off for the car and grabbed onto the bumper just as the car began to accelerate. We reached the car at the same time and hung on for dear life. The car took us down and up Sibley Hill. The ride was smooth, easy, and exuberant!

"How long should we stay on, Bruce?" I questioned.

"Just for a couple of more blocks," he said as he smiled at me. "This is great! We won't have to walk anymore. I can be over to your house in just a few minutes now!"

We let go of the bumper at the same time and slid to a stop.

"Man that was fun, Bruce! Let's hop another one back to Sib. Okay?" Sib was a nickname we used for Sibley Park. We hopped another car and got a free ride back to the top of Sibley Hill where we started. The drivers never knew we were there.

For the next few weeks, we hopped cars with the teenage boys in our neighborhood. At first they didn't want us around, but when they saw we were as good as they were, they didn't seem to mind us being there. It got to be so much fun that Bruce and I hopped cars all over t he city when the streets were packed with snow. I got to be very good at it. In fact, I once hopped a car that was going about twenty miles per hour. I dove for its bumper and dragged myself up to my feet. This dangerous pastime became especially hazardous when we hit a bare spot on the street. Bruce and I learned this lesson the hard way. We were sliding behind a car when suddenly our boots stopped sliding. We had hit a bare spot and both of us went tumbling down the street. Fortunately, we just got a little skinned up.

One night as we were waiting for cars to come by Sibley Hill, an older teenager with a very hot car stopped and asked, "What do you guys think you're doing?" He knew exactly what we were doing. "So you think you're good at hopping cars, do you? Well, get on to the back of mine!" We couldn't believe it. He actually wanted us to hop his car. We all jumped on the back of his car. I got the best spot. It was right in the center of the car. I didn't like to be behind the exhaust pipe. A bigger teenager pulled me off and said it was his spot. Every spot I picked, someone kicked me out. I wanted to be a part of that joy ride. When all the spots were picked, I grabbed the fender of the car. I had never done that before and didn't realize how dangerous it was. Another teenage boy jumped onto the running board just as the car took off. I have never been on a ride like that one in all my life! The driver swerved from side to side deliberately trying to knock us off. The boy who jumped on the running board was hanging on for dear life. The driver kept opening and closing his door and finally shook the kid off. I saw kids falling off and kids flying into snow banks as this maniac spun his car all over the road. He was able to shake everyone off his car except me. He didn't know I was hanging onto his fender until I let go. When it was over, my heart was pounding so hard that I thought it would burst. Not until later did I realize how dangerous and stupid this was.

The neighbors didn't appreciate us hopping cars and called the police. I saw a squad car coming down the street and began nonchalantly walking toward home. The squad car pulled over and shined its spotlight into my face. I heard a deep voice saying, "Come over here, Son."

I walked over to the squad car and said, "Yes, Officer. What is it?"

"Are you the one who is hopping cars?"

"No, Officer," I responded.

"Well, you'd better get home because its getting a little late for you to be out," said the policeman.

"Okay," I said and headed straight for my house.

I did, however, learn my lesson one day. I wanted to go over to Bruce's house when a Dayton's delivery truck drove by. Dayton's was a department store in downtown Minneapolis. These trucks delivered small packages all over the city. They were not even a challenge to hop because they were large van type trucks with a big bumper sticking out in back. I watched as the driver stopped at a house to deliver a package. I walked alongside the truck as the driver got in and hopped on the back of the truck completely out of the driver's view. I remember I was wearing my chopper mittens. These were the warmest mittens ever invented. My dad used to take us to Kaplin's Surplus Store and buy chopper mittens for my brothers and me. These mittens were made of cowhide with wool liners inside. No one had cold hands with these mittens on. Mom put my name, address, and phone number on the back of each mitten in case I lost them. About a half block from Bruce's house, I decided to get off. When I let go, however, my mittens stuck to the bumper of the truck. I stood dumbfounded looking at my bare hands. I knew I was in big trouble now. The driver would see my mittens and call the police with my name, and I would be off to jail. Just as I was about to cry, I saw the truck stop to make a delivery about half a block away. I took off as fast as my legs would carry me. I saw the driver coming out of the house. He started his truck just as I was about to retrieve my mittens. I was too late! I sat down in the street and cried. Then, I saw the truck stop again. I took off like a shot bound and determined to get my mittens back. I failed again. I chased this truck for four blocks until I thought my lungs would burst. I finally gave up and went home.

A few days later as I was leaving for school, Mom asked, "Where are your mittens, Tommy?"

"I don't know, Mom," I lied. "I haven't been able to find them for the last couple of days." I lied because I didn't want Mom to find out we were hopping cars. I was also living in fear and expecting a police car to pull up to my house any day. "I hope you haven't lost them. Because if you have, you will not get another pair this winter!" she stated firmly.

The following Saturday while I was skating at the park, I saw a teenager wearing my mittens. I skated by him and noticed my name, address, and phone number were blotted out. I tapped him on the shoulder and asked, "Does your dad work for Dayton's Department Store?" "Why, yes! But, how did you know?" he said.

"I don't know. Just a lucky guess," I said as I skated away.

A Strained Friendship

My last year at Standish school was very interesting. Bruce and I were again in the same class together. Our educational experience was a disaster. We went through five teachers in one year, and none of them could handle our particular class. Our classroom was bedlam. Our original teacher, Miss Foster, left after the first month of school because of a family emergency. The long-term substitute teacher had very little discipline or control, so us kids dominated her completely. I was one of the worst offenders and very difficult on my teachers. Finally, our original teacher, Miss Foster, came back and finished the year with some structure.

This was also a year of many changes. Bruce became a very popular leader. Everyone wanted to be his friend. He was growing taller and was very good looking. The girls really began to notice him. Bruce and I were still good friends, but this new popularity of his pushed me into the background. We began talking to girls more too. They became our friends in class and on the playground. Two new girls moved into our school. They were twins and they were beautiful. Their names were Marlene and Pauline. Bruce started to 'go' with Marlene. Suddenly, it became important to have a girlfriend. I wasn't as quick to jump in because I felt awkward around girls and didn't quite know how to respond. Bruce had no problem. He adapted to the change quite nicely. In fact, he rather enjoyed all the attention he received from the opposite sex.

Toward the end of the year, Judy Johnson gave a party. It was the first party for boys and girls I had ever been invited to. There were about eight boys and eight girls invited to this party.

"What are you wearing to the party, Bruce?" I asked.

"I don't know. Probably just slacks and a nice shirt," he said.

"Will you pick me up on your way tomorrow night?" I asked.

"I'd really like to, Hallsey, but I already promised Marlene I would go with her," he said.

"That's okay. I'll see you there tomorrow."

I went to the party with Terry, Butch, and a couple of other friends. Judy met us at the door. "Hi, guys! Come on in. We're all downstairs."

We walked downstairs. Everyone was sitting on the floor listening to music. At first things moved rather slowly. Everyone felt awkward except for Bruce and Marlene. They seemed to be very comfortable with each other and were always together. As the evening wore on, we all began to mix more freely.

"Hey, I've got a suggestion," said Marlene. "Let's play Spin the Bottle." Everyone seemed to think it was a great idea. I wasn't exactly sure what Spin the Bottle was until we started playing. Then, I caught on in a hurry. Marlene spun the bottle, and it pointed to Bruce. The two of them went into the next room and were in there for quite awhile. When they came out, they both had huge smiles on their faces. As we played, I prayed the bottle would never point to me. I had never kissed a girl in my whole life. I wanted to run. Fortunately, it did not point to me for quite a long time. Everyone seemed to enjoy this game. Finally, Judy spun the bottle and it pointed to me. I turned red! Everyone laughed and said, "It's your turn, Tommy." I slowly got up and walked into the next room with Judy. The lights were out, and I didn't exactly know what to do. We just stood and looked at each other in the dark for a period of time which seemed like an eternity to me. She didn't say anything, so I picked up her hand, kissed it, and ran out of the room.

After that party many of my friends had girlfriends. For some reason this was difficult for me. I wasn't ready yet. I felt so uncomfortable with girls that I didn't attend another coed party until I was in high school.

As Bruce's image increased with the girls, he also became a

leader with the boys. He seemed to have it all. He was good looking, athletic, and tough. Our friendship began to change as he spent more time with friends who wanted to be around girls.

Our times together started revolving mainly around sports. This was an area in which we both excelled! Although Bruce was more of a natural athlete, I was competitive, determined, and would never give up. We both loved sports so much that our time together in this area was unstrained and natural. However, when the practices and games were over, things began to change drastically.

One evening after football practice Bruce said, "Let's go down to Tony's grocery store after practice!"

"Sounds great," everyone piped in. After practice we all walked down to Tony's Store, which was two blocks from the park on busy Thirty-Eighth Street. Tony's was a place where we often met. We would buy candy and just hang out. When we got there, Bruce pulled out a pack of cigarettes. It was a pack of Lucky Strikes. He lit up a cigarette and began puffing on it. He looked cool as he blew the smoke slowly out of his mouth. "Do you want one, Hall?" he said as he tipped the pack so one cigarette stuck out above the others.

Bruce no longer called me Tommy but Hallsey or Hall, which is my last name. I now called him "Wakes", which was short for Wakefield. I looked at him for a brief moment and was kind of stunned. I didn't want to turn him down, but I didn't want to smoke either. Before I could give him an answer, the other guys all said, "We'll take one, Wakes." We sat around and talked for about an hour. Everyone had about two or three cigarettes. Everyone, that is, except me! For the first time in my life, I felt uncomfortable around Bruce and the rest of my friends. Bruce never pushed cigarettes on me or offered one to me again. He respected me enough not to make me feel bad, even though I was the only one in our group who did not smoke. Going to Tony's after practice and having a smoke became a regular activity. Everyone seemed to enjoyed this time together and the new adventure with tobacco. Everyone, except me. The more smoking the gang did, the bolder everyone became. Soon many of the guys walked to practice smoking cigarettes. It became part of our image.

One day after practice, we all went to Tony's for a smoke.

When we were ready to leave, I said to Bruce, "Light me up a cigarette." He looked at me kind of strangely for a second. Then, without batting an eye he pulled a cigarette out, lit it up, and handed it to me. As we walked home, I felt part of the group carrying the cigarette in my right hand. When I separated from the guys and walked toward my house, I threw the cigarette on the ground without puffing it even once. I wanted to be a part of the group so much. But, for some strange reason, I just couldn't begin smoking.

As sixth grade wore on, my friends began to change. I wasn't invited to the parties with the rest of the guys. I began to hang around Sibley Park a lot more often. Terry was down at the park all the time, so we began to hang around together. He wasn't into girls or smoking either. He loved sports as much as I did and was a very good athlete. He was not as natural as Bruce but worked hard at everything he did. His father had been our football coach when we were fifth graders. Terry and I began to spend a lot of time together.

One fall night when Terry and I were shooting baskets under the lights, Bruce came to the park with about six of his friends.

"Wanna get a game up, Hall?" he said as they walked toward us.

"Sure, Wakes! That is, if it's all right with you, Terry?" I said.

"It's all right with me," he said.

"All right! You, Terry, John, and Mike will play against us four," Bruce started taking the leadership as usual to get things going. I noticed for the first time that Bruce and I were not on the same team. "You guys can have the ball first. We'll play half-court rules. Every time the ball changes hands, you must take it back to the free throw line," he continued. "If anyone fouls, it's up to the person to admit it. If nothing is said, the game goes on."

Our team circled around each other to decide which man to cover. "I'll take Bruce," I said.

"Okay," said Terry. "But if he scores too many points off of you, I'll switch with you. Okay?"

We played for about an hour. It was a tough physical game. Bruce and I really went after each other. When I drove to the net and he fouled me, he called a foul. Bruce was very fair. Many times he stuffed me and shut me down. He and I were tough competitors, especially against one another. However, the deep respect and love that we had for each other still remained, even though our lives were beginning to move in different directions. They beat us in a close game.

"Nice game, Tommy," said Bruce as he stuck out his hand to shake mine.

"Yeah, nice game, Bruce," I said.

"You guys a little thirsty?" he said.

"Yeah, my throat feels like cotton," I responded.

"Well, we've got a little refreshment over in the bushes," he said as he walked toward them with all the guys following. When we got there, Bruce walked into the middle of a bush and came out with a case of beer. He opened a bottle and began drinking. "This sure tastes good after a tough game."

Bruce's friends all rushed in and grabbed a bottle. "Do you want one, Hall?" he said. Even though I was dying of thirst, it didn't seem right. I looked over at Terry.

He said, "I'm going back to the drinking fountain, Tom. Water quenches my thirst better than beer."

"Wait, Terry. I'll go with you," I said. "Thanks for the game, Bruce. We'll see you guys later," I said as I walked back to the park with Terry.

"Thanks, Terry, for getting me off the hook," I said. "I didn't want to drink beer with those guys either but didn't quite know what to say."

"I'm not drinking, Tom! Not for Bruce or anyone else. I want to be good at sports. Drinking will catch up with those guys sooner or later."

"Did you know they were drinking?" I said. "I knew they smoked a lot but hadn't heard that they were actually drinking."

"Yeah! Everyone knows those guys drink. You can't hide that for very long. Where have you been, Tommy?" said Terry.

"I guess I heard that they were, but I had to see it to believe it. Anyway, it was easier for me to refuse with you here. Thanks, Terry!"

"That's okay. I'm not going to drink or smoke for any reason or for anybody," said Terry very confidently. I was glad I had found a friend with such a strong conviction.

A Period of Change

Bruce was right! Junior high proved to be a time of many changes. We enrolled in Folwell Junior High as seventh graders in the fall of 1952. Folwell School was much different than elementary school. This school was a three story building just four blocks from my home. Bruce lived farther away and had a much longer walk. On the first day we all met in the auditorium for our introduction. I found Bruce and some other friends and sat with them. The principal came onto the stage and stepped up to the microphone. His name was Mr. Keck. He wore a dark suit and looked very proper and distinguished with his gray hair and glasses. I wondered if Miss Psalm had sent my record file over to him about my years at Standish. I was scared and nervous about this new venture in junior high. Everything seemed so much bigger and more complicated.

"Welcome to Folwell Junior High," he said. "I'm sure you'll enjoy your new school. It will be a lot different from your elementary school. You'll meet new friends and have several teachers throughout the day. The counselors will hand out your schedules according to your last name. Each of you will be given a homeroom and a locker. You report to your homeroom during the first hour every day. Announcements are given at this time. Then, you follow your schedule throughout the day. Please come to the front of the auditorium to receive your schedules. A through H"s will be on my right, and over to my left will be I's through Z. Are there any questions?" He paused and looked around.

"Well, if there are no questions then you may go to the appropriate area to pick-up your schedule."

"I guess we go to opposite sides of the auditorium, Bruce," I said as we walked out of our aisle and moved toward the front.

"Yeah, I hope this doesn't mean that we won't see each other throughout the day," Bruce said as we inched our way to the front. "After you get your schedule, let's check to see if we have any classes together, Tommy."

"Okay, I'll meet you in the hall right outside the auditorium." After I received my schedule, I met Bruce in the hallway. We compared our schedules. Not only were we not in any classes together, but our homerooms were totally apart from each other. My homeroom and locker were on the first floor, and his were on the third floor.

"Oh well, Tommy. We'll see each other down at the park after school," he said as he walked up the stairs to meet his homeroom teacher.

I guess we both adjusted to our new environment alright. However, our school was so big that I never saw Bruce throughout the day. We did play football together at Sib and had a great season together. But, that was the extent of our relationship that autumn. We both were making new friends. My friends hung around the park all the time, and now Bruce mostly came there just for practices and games. Otherwise, I never saw him. He went to parties and hung out with girls a lot. We did not share that common interest yet. I was still very shy around girls.

On Friday nights Sibley Park sponsored dances for junior high kids in the main park building. Bruce and his friends never missed a dance. I always saw him walking into the dances while I played half-court basketball with my friends outside under the lights. One Friday night as I walked home carrying my basketball, I stopped and looked in the window of the main building. I saw all the kids dancing together and looked for Bruce. He was over in the corner dancing with a girl I had never seen before. I stood and watched through the window for a long time. I did not have the slightest idea how to dance, but it did look like a lot of fun.

Bruce and I still talked when we saw each other, but we both could tell things had changed. We were heading in two different directions and didn't hang out anymore. However, we did still come together in sports. We always played on the same football, hockey, and baseball teams. In football, I played quarterback and he played fullback. In hockey, I played center and he played right wing. And in baseball, I played left field and he played third base.

Our greatest love was hockey. In seventh grade my older brother, Dave, coached us in hockey. Dave didn't go to college right away but worked as an iron worker. He saved his money for college so he could become a teacher and coach. Dave loved hockey and was a very good coach. Because he was seven years older than me and since I was his brother, Dave was very hard on me. He expected me to perform at my top level all the time. The other kids loved him, but I struggled with his strictness.

The park board ran a very good hockey program. Junior high kids played midgets, and many kids tried out for the team. Dave cut the squad down to fifteen players. Bruce, Terry, and I made the first line. That was something since the second line was all eighth graders. We scrimmaged in practices and continually beat them even though they were older and stronger than us. Terry, Bruce, and I were something to watch. We skated very well together, and no one could stop us. We were unselfish team players who passed to each other all the time. Dave taught us to play as a team and often said, "An assist is as good as a goal." An assist is when a player passes the puck to another player who scores the goal. We practiced every night after supper under the lights. Dave worked us very hard, and it paid off.

Terry and I hated to leave the ice. When practice was over, we always stayed until the lights went out at 9:30. Terry lived across the street, and my house was just a short block away. Bruce lived farther away so he usually left right after practice. During Christmas vacation Terry and I skated from morning to night. I didn't even like to go home for lunch. Instead, I sent my brothers home to get me a sandwich and an orange. Bruce came once in a while. With our hard work and determination, Terry and I almost caught up to Bruce's natural ability. Bruce was still a dominant player and awesome to watch. He was not a hog, though, and we worked together very well.

Terry became a good friend of mine. He wasn't into girls, smoking, or drinking either. He was outspoken, determined, and a tough competitor. He was small, tough, and wiry with brown hair and a slender build. Terry was very fast. He never gave up or quit. I think we both made each other better players.

Terry and I met every day at the skating rink. When it snowed, we helped the custodian shovel the rink. We also went down to the park early in the morning and helped him flood the rink. The custodian's name was Elmer. We became good friends with Elmer. He enjoyed our company and help. In fact, when we were high school players, Elmer never missed one of our games at the Dupont Arena.

One Saturday morning I walked down to the rink just as Elmer was dragging the hoses out to flood the rink.

"Hi, Elmer. Could you use a little help?" I asked.

"Sure, Tommy! Let's get this hose in the rink," he said. The hose was about three times bigger than a garden hose in diameter and four times as long. It was kept in the basement of the main building so it wouldn't freeze up. The hose had to be dragged in and out every morning to put on a fresh coat of ice.

Elmer was a kind man with a soft heart. He was older, maybe in his late fifties. He always wore large coveralls that zipped in the front. His boots were lined with white sheep fur. He wore a gray hat with a short visor in the front. It kind of looked like a golfer's hat. If it got really cold, he put the flappers down to cover his ears. Once in a while he bought us a candy bar and a coke after we helped him flood the rink.

Elmer's flooding technique was a real art. He would flood a section of ice, and I would drag the hose over it to smooth it out. We worked around the rink and made a smooth sheet of ice that shined like glass in the cold winter sun.

"Elmer, you make the best ice in the city," I said. "I've skated at a lot of parks, and no one has smooth ice like we do."

"Thanks, Tommy! When I see you kids skating as much as you do, it makes it all worthwhile," he said with a twinkle in his eye.

"You know, Elmer, I don't just skate in the hockey rink. I use the big rink as well. I just love to skate. There is no feeling like it in the world. It's almost like flying. I just wish I could skate as well as Bruce Wakefield, that's all," I said.

"You know, Tommy, I've been watching you and think you and he are pretty close."

"Do you really think so, Elmer?" I questioned.

"I sure do, Tommy. Oh, I'll admit he has a powerful stride and is very smooth, but don't shortchange yourself. You are quick and can cut on a dime," Elmer said confidently. "I would just as soon watch you skate as anyone down here."

I don't know whether what Elmer said was true or not, but he did give me confidence and encouraged me a lot. I really loved that man! I never knew much about his family but sensed that he had had a difficult life. He was a neat person and worked very hard to give us kids a good ice surface each and every day. In high school I always looked for him sitting at the far end of the Arena with one of his custodian friends cheering for our hockey team.

Our midget hockey team won the district sectional playoffs. My brother and some of the parents drove us all over the city to play our games. One of our toughest games came when we traveled down to Riverside Park. They had an excellent team. The score was two to two after two periods. Their team was very physical and hard hitting. They had two brothers who played very well together. Their names were Rick and Tim Alm. When we got into the warming house after the second period, Dave got us together in the corner and gave us a pep talk. As I took off my skates to warm my feet, I looked up in amazement. Their defenseman, who had been knocking me all over the ice, took off her stocking cap and shook out her hair. It was a girl! I nudged Bruce.

"Look at their defenseman! She's a girl!"

"I can't believe it!" he said. "She's not only very good, but she's tough!"

"Yeah!" I said, "And if we don't keep our heads up around her, we'll be flat on our backs. What's her name, Terry?"

"Her name is Judy Wesby," he said. "She's Jim Wesby's sister." The Wesby and Alm families had great hockey players. They grew up around Riverside Park. They eventually went to South High, and we played some great games against them in high school.

Terry, Bruce, and I were on the ice during the final minutes of our game. There was a face-off in the center of the rink. I drew the puck back to our defenseman. He passed the puck over to Terry. Terry skated up the ice and passed it to me. I skated up the ice with Bruce on my right side. Judy Wesby was between Bruce and me. I knew she wanted to check me. I skated close to her and, just as she hit me, slid the puck over to Bruce. He drove to the net and scored as I flew into the corner on my butt.

He came over and picked me up and said, "Nice pass, Tommy! Nice pass!"

We won the game three to two and were headed for the city championship. We practiced hard for a week before the big game. Finally, the night of the game came. We met down at Sib. Dave got us together in the warming house and said, "Well, guys, tonight we play for the city championship! We've worked hard all year, and I hope we can go out a winner. Give it all you've got because there is no tomorrow. Has everyone got a ride?" he asked. "I'll take Bruce, Tommy, and Terry in my car. We'll meet at Lynhurst Park."

When we got to the park, we noticed a lot of people there. We went into the warming house and laced up our skates. Bruce helped me tighten my skates. "I'm nervous, Bruce," I said. "Look at those guys! They're huge!"

"I've got the butterflies too!" he admitted. "We'll just have to play our game, and we'll be alright."

We walked out of the warming house and skated to the hockey rink. People were standing all around the rink. We skated around the rink a couple of times to get loosened up. Then, we warmed up our goalie by taking some shots at him. The referee blew the whistle, and we skated over to our coach. "This is it, guys! It's for all the marbles. Play with all your heart and work together," said Dave.

We all put our hands together and shouted, "Let's go!" I skated to the center of the ice to take the face-off! I looked up at their center who was about five inches taller than me. He looked down at me and made a mean face. The ref dropped the puck and the game began. They were big, fast, and good. They were by far the best team we had ever played. They scored a quick goal and were off to a flying start. After the first period, we were losing five to nothing. We skated into the warming house hanging our heads. We had a little time between each period because they shoveled the rink by hand to clear the snow.

We sat down on the bench and loosened our skates. Dave began speaking to us, "We're down by five goals, but we can skate with them. I don't want you guys giving up. Keep plugging away and the goals will come."

"What do you think, Bruce?" I said. "We haven't been behind

in a game all season."

"They're good, Tommy. But, if you can get me the puck, I think I can score," he said confidently.

"I can get you the puck alright. You just put it in the net. Okay?"

I put my arm around Terry and said, "How are you doing?"

"I'm okay," he said. "I'm just a little shell shocked, that's all."

"We can do it, Terry!" I said. "We're not going down without a fight."

We looked over at the other team. They were already celebrating their victory. "Look at them, Bruce," I said. "They think the game is over, and we still have two periods to play!"

"No way, Tommy! Just get me that puck!" he said with a determined look in his eye.

I had seen that look in Bruce's eye before and knew this game was far from over. Before we started the second period, my brother said, "The first period was theirs, but this one is ours. The second line has played them even. But, Tommy, your line has to start putting the puck in the net. Now go get them!"

The second period of the game began. There was a loose puck which Terry picked up and passed over to me. I skated up the rink and went around an opposing player. I looked up and saw Bruce streaking down the right side of the rink. I drilled a pass to him, and he drove in and scored. The goal judge raised his hand. We finally broke the ice, and it was a hard fought second period. When it was over, the score was five to three. Bruce had scored two goals, and I had scored one.

Things were different in the warming house after the second period. The smiles and celebration were no longer on the faces of the opposing team. They now knew they were in a game!

"That was a great second period, guys!" my brother said. "We're still down by two goals, but now we have the momentum. Don't let up! Keep the pressure on and let out all the stops in the final period."

"Bruce, that first goal you got was beautiful. It really got us going." "I could never have done it without that nice pass from you!" he said. "Tommy, I want this game. We can beat this team. I know we can!"

"Bruce, you just keep moving to open ice, and I'll see that you get the puck. I want this game as much as you do, and we're going to get it!" I said just as determined as Bruce.

"Terry, keep pumping. We're not done yet," I said. "You'll get a goal. Just keep going hard for the net."

"I don't care if I score or not, Tommy!" he said. "I just want to win this game."

In the third period, they really came at us. They were bigger and more physical than we were and were knocking us off the puck. Finally, there was a scramble in front of the net. I grabbed the loose puck and drilled one into the upper right-hand corner. The score was five to four with four minutes left in the game. During the next shift, I was skating hard up the ice when their big defenseman nailed me with a solid check. Bruce slid over and picked up the loose puck. Two opposing players tore after him. They were not going to let him score again and converged on him quickly. He passed the puck behind his back to Terry who swooped in to score the tieing goal. Our team went crazy! The game was tied with two minutes left on the clock.

As we changed lines, I grabbed Terry and said, "Nice goal! Nice goal!"

"Did you see that pass from Wakes?" he said. "It was behind his back."

I looked over at Bruce, and he just winked. The referee blew his whistle, and we skated out on the ice for the final minute of the game. I looked at their big center who didn't look so big anymore. The referee dropped the puck. I pushed it between the big center's legs and picked it up on the other side of him. We were on a break. Terry and Bruce were skating hard right with me. I crossed the blue line and passed it to Terry. He drove for the goal but was cut off. He dropped it back to me. I faked a shot and slid it over to Bruce who jammed it into the net. We scored! Bruce, Terry, and I hugged each other. We had won the Midget City Championship. We had done it together. It was a team effort. We came back from a five goal deficit, and now we were the city champions from Sibley Park!

Tom

Bruce

Terry

Kempter

Everyone liked Mr. Kempter. He was our gym teacher at Folwell Junior High. He not only taught gym but built character in all our lives. The students at Folwell came from three elementary schools. Some students were very rough and came from tough neighborhoods. Mr. Kempter could handle any kind of student. His classes were very organized. He was a strong disciplinarian, but he loved his job as well as his students. The kids all called him Kemp. He ran an intramural sporting program after school where homerooms played against other homerooms. He used the ninth graders to referee. These games were really a big deal. We could also earn points to get a letter in ninth grade. It was a real status symbol to have a sweater with the letter 'F' on it. The 'F' stood for Folwell Junior High School. This was the only time I remember where the letter 'F' meant something very special.

Bruce and I played in all the intramural games after school. Bruce's homeroom team won the seventh grade basketball championship. My homeroom didn't do so well, but Kemp noticed I was a pretty good athlete. He told me to try out for the tumbling class as an eighth grader. Each year Kemp picked the best tumblers to be in his tumbling class. The class consisted of eighth and ninth grade boys who worked all year on gymnastic skills. This tumbling class put on a school assembly and amazed me with their performance. They did diving rolls, front and back handsprings, cartwheels, and front and back flips on the trampoline. I wanted to be in the class. I worked on some of the skills in the summer and during my eighth grade year was picked to be in this class. Bruce was also selected. I looked forward to this tumbling gym class every day. We always had to change into our gym clothes which were white shorts, a tee-shirt, and tennis shoes. To begin class we stood on numbers around the gym while Kemp gave some announcements and warmed us up. Then we practiced tumbling stunts. I learned to do many of the tumbling activities. I even walked on my hands. I also worked the trampoline and did front and back flips. Bruce was a very good tumbler too. He could even do a running front flip.

Mr. Kempter ran a pretty tight ship. His classes were large, so he didn't like kids fooling around. Also, there were some pretty rough kids in this class. Some of them were Greasers. Greasers were tough kids who wore their hair long and put grease in their hair. It wasn't actually grease but lots of hair oil. They combed their hair to make a duck-tail. A duck-tail was when the back hair on each side was combed toward the middle making a part down the center. Greasers wore leather jackets and hung around together. They were discipline problems and gave teachers a hard time. That is every teacher except Mr. Kempter. No one gave him a hard time!

During gym class one day, Curtie Steen was showing Jack Hamilton how to comb his hair into a duck-tail. We were supposed to be working on our tumbling skills and were not permitted back in the locker room until gym class was over. Mr. Kempter walked into the locker room and saw these two boys. They were the toughest kids in our school. Mr. Kempter grabbed them by the hair and brought them to the middle of the gym floor. He blew his whistle, and we all stopped as he threw a fit!

"Look at this!" he screamed. "Grease!" He slid his hands together and said again, "Grease! These pretty boys were in the locker room during gym class combing their hair with grease." He pushed the two boys against the wall and screamed in their faces, "You never leave this gymnasium again! Is that clear? Especially not to comb your hair with grease!" I couldn't believe it, but Jack and Curt were scared to death. Actually, so were the rest of us. No one ever crossed Mr. Kempter and got away with it. Jack and Curt always picked fights and hurt kids in our school. No one had stood up to them until now. Mr. Kempter had treated them fairly until they crossed him. Believe me, they never crossed Kempter again. He used a very severe tactic on these two boys, but no teacher could handle them or make them behave. That was until now!

Mr. Kempter was always having contests. One day after class began he said, "Alright. I want everyone up on their hands. If you fall, you must sit down. We'll see who can stand on their hands the longest." There were forty in our class. It must have been a strange sight, but we all were walking on our hands. One by one we fell down until there were only two kids left standing on their hands. One was Bruce Wakefield and the other was Russ Anderson. They kept walking all over the gym. Finally, Mr. Kempter said, "Okay, that's enough. You're both winners." Everyone clapped and once again I was impressed with Bruce's athletic ability.

That spring we put on a tumbling show for the school and the community. It was on a Thursday, and I invited my parents. I couldn't believe it when both Mom and Dad said they would come. The auditorium was packed as we began our performance. Mats were lined up across the stage. We did forward and backward rolls, cartwheels, and back extensions. We even did diving rolls. One ninth grader dove over seven kids who were kneeling on the floor. Then, eight kids knelt down so the smallest kid in the class could dive over all of them! The audience held their breath as he came running full-speed down the mats. He leaped into the air, and we all turned over quickly and caught him in mid-air. The audience roared! I did front and back flips on the trampoline. Bruce and three other boys walked across the stage on their hands. Mom told me later that Dad really enjoyed the show. He was afraid when I was doing flips on the trampoline that my teeth would fall out though.

Even though he was a very strict teacher, Mr. Kempter liked both Bruce and me. I thought he would never discipline me. As usual, I learned my lesson the hard way. We were outside playing flag football when I picked up some small stones on the playground. For some dumb reason, I threw them out into the street. Just then Mr. Kempter blew his whistle and said, "Everybody in!" Then he added, "I want the person who was throwing stones to report to me!" We all ran back into the building. When I ran by Mr. Kempter, he grabbed me by the shoulder and said, "You weren't going to tell me! Were you, Tommy?" He hung on to my shoulder and marched me into his office. Then, he pulled down the shades. He did this when he was really upset with someone. No one wanted to be in his office when he pulled down the shades. No one ever told what he said or did when they were in his office. And no one wanted to find out either! I was shaking and was so scared that I couldn't even talk. Then, he proceeded to chew me out and build me up at the same time.

"Tom, I thought that I could trust you. When you ran by me, I was very disappointed! When you do something wrong, and it will happen again, never ever be so hard as to not confess. Be a man and take your punishment. Tommy, you're one of my best students. I couldn't believe it when I saw you throwing stones. Then, I even gave you a chance to confess, but you thought you could get away with it. Didn't you?"

"Yes, Sir," I said. "I don't know why I threw the stones. I guess I just wasn't thinking."

"Those small stones are what our playground is made of. We can't have them all over the street. You will miss gym for a week, and you will take a broom and sweep all the little stones up from the street. Report to Mr. Keck's office during gym class for the next week."

"Mr. Kempter, your discipline is fair," I said. "But, I hope you'll forgive me. I promise I won't let you down again."

After I swept the street and served my time in Mr. Keck's office, Mr. Kempter acted like it never had happened. I respected him more than any teacher I've ever had. You know, I'll never forget that talk for as long as I live!

Mr. Kempter was a man of principle and character. He was way ahead of his time. He taught his students the value of a good attitude. He helped build solid character traits into their lives. He taught things like being true to your word, honesty, and hard work. He turned many lives around that were headed in the wrong direction during his long extended career. I appreciate this man and what he taught me about life.

An Embarrassing Experience

It all started quite slowly. First, there was a small pimple. Then, there were two. Before I knew what was happening, my face was covered with acne. I also began to trip over my own feet. I felt awkward in social situations and especially around girls. As this attraction for girls began to emerge, so did my feelings of inadequacy. I began to withdraw. I had a strange feeling my eighth grade year would be a difficult journey. Little did I know how true that would be.

Something very unexpected happened one day, and I was not prepared to handle it. It not only drew attention to me but alerted the whole school as to who I was. I had become very self-conscious. I thought people were looking at me, and I didn't want to do anything to draw attention to myself. The very thing I tried to avoid came to me like a bad dream. I had an extremely strict history teacher. Her name was Miss Pankonen. She wanted total silence in her classroom, and she got it! I tiptoed in her classroom and wondered if I tiptoed too loudly. My most embarrassing moment occurred in her classroom, and by the end of the day the whole school knew about it.

I sat in her class during fourth period, which was right after lunch. I had eaten a chicken sandwich for lunch that day. Some meat got stuck between my teeth and really bothered me. I didn't know what to do until I spotted a rubber band around my notebook. I remembered seeing Dad use this tool to clean his teeth at home. This was before the days of dental floss. I waited until Miss Pankonen turned to write on the chalkboard with her back to the class. I very carefully and quietly took the band off the book. Then, I stretched the rubber band between my teeth to remove the piece of unwanted meat. All of a sudden — fling!!!

My false teeth shot out of my mouth! Everything suddenly seemed to slow down. It was like watching an instant replay of a sporting event. I saw my teeth flying through the air! I felt a rush of blood slowly fill my face as it heated up like a hot air balloon. I was shocked, helpless, and frightened all at the same time. I watched my teeth as they flew high above the classroom and headed straight for Susan.

Susan was a girl I had an incredible crush on but was too embarrassed to tell anyone. She had long silky black hair. Her smile would light up a room, and she could melt me with just a quick glance. Susan, however, did not know I even existed. I was too shy to even talk to her. I thought she was out of my league! Now, she was about to be introduced to a part of me that was way too up front and personal.

Susan felt something hit her back. She looked down and saw my teeth on the floor. I panicked when I saw she was going to pick them up. I could just hear her say, "Who lost their teeth?" So, I dove for my teeth sending my chair and books flying! I crawled on my hands and knees with lightening speed and reached my teeth just before Susan picked them up. Our eyes met briefly as I quickly placed my teeth back into my mouth. I'll never forget the strange look on her face as she tried to assess the whole situation.

The class was in a total uproar! Miss Pankonen wheeled around and glared at me sitting on the floor with my face totally flushed and in a state of shock! She asked for an explanation. I told her I needed to talk to her out in the hall.

"Fine!" she shouted. "Go out in the hall! This better be good!"

Miss Pankonen listened intently as I explained the whole story. I'm sure in all her thirty years of teaching she had never heard a story quite like this one. She was starting to smile, so she turned her back to me and said, "Make sure this never happens again!" No one had ever seen Miss Pankonen smile! But, I know she was smiling then!

The kids in my fourth hour class could hardly wait for the

period to be over. The story spread like wildfire throughout the student body and, I imagine, among the faculty as well. Now, everyone in the whole school knew I had false teeth!

A Terrible Tragedy

My family went to church in the morning and had just finished a delicious meal. Mom cooked Dad's favorite meatloaf and mashed potatoes with 'Brucey Gravy.' My father wasn't feeling well. He decided to take a nap, which he rarely did. I was feeling very full and satisfied when my friend, John, rang our doorbell. John was a good friend, and I was glad to see him.

"Tom, do you want to find something to do this afternoon?"
"Sure, John. What do you have in mind?"

"Let's go over to Joan's house and see what's happening."

We were at the age when we were getting interested in girls but still were a little awkward with our emotions and feelings. He wanted me to go with him to see his girlfriend. He felt a little more secure with someone along. That Sunday afternoon was a clear, sunny, spring day. I went with John. We spent a couple of hours at Joan's house and had a good time just talking together.

When we returned home, John and I saw several cars parked in front of my house.

"John, that's really strange to see all that company at our house. My dad wasn't even feeling well this morning!"

"There sure are a lot of cars, Tom. I wonder what's going on?"

When we got to the back porch, my sister, Gwen, met us at the door. I saw she was crying. Her eyes were red and wet tears streamed down her face.

"What's the matter, Gwen?"

Her eyes filled with pain and looked deep into mine as she

92

said, "Dad died this afternoon, Tommy!"

I couldn't believe what I was hearing, but her eyes told me it was true. I don't know what happened next. I may have gone into shock or something, but I found myself in my bedroom crying without realizing how I got there. As I tried to process what had happened, the tears kept flooding my eyes. I wept and wept. I don't know how long this went on, but I woke up the next morning totally spent. At first I thought it was all a bad dream, but then I realized it was true.

I went downstairs where everyone was sober and quiet. Mom told me Dad had a massive heart attack. She said, "If the doctor had been standing right next to him, he couldn't have saved him. He got out of bed and just dropped on the living room floor." The next few days were a living nightmare. I felt so empty and sad that I didn't want to go on living. So many times I wanted to talk to Dad and apologize for causing him so much pain. Now, it was too late. I tested the limits all the time, and he had to discipline me continually. I didn't know what to do because I had so much guilt and couldn't release it. Everyone in my family was suffering, but I felt totally isolated.

My father had a huge funeral. Many people came to see Dad. He had touched many lives, and I heard people talking about what a great man he was. I went up to the casket and looked at him for a long time. I told him I was sorry for not being an obedient son. I asked him to forgive me. Then, I touched his body! His skin was hard, brittle, and cold. I knew he wasn't there any longer. I believed he was a Christian and was in heaven. I missed him already and wondered how Mom would make it with five boys to raise. My sister was married, and my older brother was to be married the next month. I was now the oldest at home at age fourteen. I was not prepared for, nor did I want, that responsibility.

We received many cards and letters with money in them. Our neighbors, friends, and relatives were very generous. Dad had a life insurance policy which paid up the mortgage on our house. However, Mom had to carry on with just his small social security check. The money problem became a real issue.

Several weeks after Dad's death, Mom went into severe depression. It seemed as if she lost her will to live. I would go to school and leave her with a blank stare on her face. She would say, "Are you coming home after school, Tommy?"

"Yes, Mom."

"That's nice."

"Mom, are you all right?"

"I'm fine. Now you run along to school."

I couldn't stand seeing her like that and tried everything I could think of to snap her out of her depression. But, it was useless and I was frightened. I didn't want to leave her because I wasn't sure she would be there when I returned home from school. She wasn't functioning properly. I thought us kids might be taken from her and our family split-up and put in a foster home or something. I kept things going for awhile but wasn't sure how long I could see her in that state of mind.

I felt awkward at school. Everyone knew about my father's death. Yet, no one said anything. Once again I felt isolated and alone with all eyes staring at me. Mr. Kempter, my gym teacher, noticed my struggle and took me into his office. This time he didn't pull down the shade, which was a good sign.

"Tell me about your dad, Tom."

"Well, Kemp, he was 54 years old," I began.

"That's a shame. That's a damn shame! That's how old I am!"

"He was a good man, Kemp. He worked hard and really loved my mom. She misses him real bad, and I can't seem to cheer her up no matter what I do!"

"Do you have anyone at home to help you?"

"Yeah, my older brother and sister come over from time to time. You know, Dad was always in a good mood. He had a really infectious laugh. He would tell a joke then laugh so hard that we all laughed at his laugh and not his joke. I can still see his face laughing. It's so clear in my mind. I loved him, Mr. Kempter, but I wasn't a very good son. Now he's gone, and I won't ever see him again. I can't even tell him I'm sorry! I feel so bad, and I don't know what to do."

Tears were running down my face, and I began to cry which I rarely did at that point in my life. Mr. Kempter helped me release my emotions that day, and I was grateful to have someone to talk to. However, I didn't talk about Dad to anyone again for a long time. I became angry and bitter and didn't work through this problem until I was in my twenties. But on that day, I thanked God for Mr. Kempter who cared enough about one of his students to reach deep inside when he was hurting.

When school was over, I rushed home to find Mom sitting in the same chair with a bleak stare in her eyes. I really hated to see her like that, but I couldn't help her. I cried and prayed to God to give Mother back to us because we needed her. This, on top of my father's death, was more than I could bear. My older brother and sister tried to help out, but they had their jobs and families to take of. So, I had to carry most of the load.

Finally one morning about two months later, I came downstairs and saw the sparkle back in Mom's eyes. I had been watching her eyes because they told the story of Mom's life. My heart leaped for joy. Mom was back! I hugged her and told her we were going to be a family again. I promised to do my part to adjust to living without Dad. She cried and said she was sorry. She now was ready to live without my father. She loved and missed him so much that she just needed to grieve until it had run its course. She realized there were five of us who needed and depended on her to continue to function as a family. There was a big hole left by Dad's death. I thanked God because I knew the long struggle was over. Mom was ready to begin to live again. I also knew my role would change drastically as four little brothers looked for leadership from me.

My ninth grade year was the most difficult year of my life. I began to struggle with acne and also broke out with a skin infection called eczema. This did not get any better, in fact it got worse, until I was out of high school. That along with my father's death put a big load on my shoulders. I was withdrawing and pulling inward.

It was a rough summer adjusting to life without a father. I was the man of the house. My dad had bought an old Studebaker for a couple hundred dollars just before he died. I wasn't old enough to have a license yet. However, I began driving the car around the block to practice for the test when I turned sixteen. My mother didn't approve of this, so I snuck the car out when she wasn't looking. I could hardly wait for my fifteenth birthday in August. Then, I could get my permit and practice legally for my license. One of my neighbors saw me driving the car and told my mother. She forbid me to drive the car until I got my permit, and then I could only drive with a licensed driver. Mom had never learned to drive a car.

Mom recovered slowly from her depression but realized life had to go on! Mom and I became very close.

"Tommy, you're going to have to be the man around the house now!" she said.

"I know, Mom," I replied.

"I don't want you to do anything that will cause your brothers to get into trouble," she said seriously. "They all look up to you!"

"I'll try, Mom, but it won't be easy! I can't wait until I can drive, Mom. I'll take you anywhere you want to go," I said. "Actually, I already know how to drive, but I'm just not old enough to take the test yet."

"That time will come soon enough," she said.

"Mom, are you scared without Dad?" I asked.

"In a way," she said with a far away look in her eyes as if she was trying to picture my dad or hang on to some memory. "He always made me feel so secure! When I went to bed at night with his big strong arms around me, I didn't have a care in the world," she continued. "But the Lord will take care of us, Tommy! You know he watches out for widows."

Mom had a strong faith. She not only believed it, she lived it! She used to embarrass me when my friends came to pick me up for school. I could never leave the house without her reading from the Bible and praying for me. This used to bother me, but it never seemed to bother my friends. They all loved and respected my mother.

I will have to admit, though, Mom had her hands full raising five boys alone. I also could never ask her for money. I began doing odd jobs around the neighborhood and caddied at the Minikahda Country Club in the summers.

Sophomores

In the fall I entered Roosevelt Senior High School. It was huge! Students from three junior high schools merged into this school. Over seven hundred kids were in our sophomore class alone. It was an exciting year. I played on the sophomore football, hockey, and baseball team. I wasn't much of a student and never took a book home to study. Still, I managed to maintain a 'C' average. Mom never pushed grades, so I didn't worry about them either. Our high school varsity basketball team won the state championship for the second year in a row.

My love was hockey however. I never missed a varsity game. They were held at the Dupont Arena. This was a large old building where the Minneapolis Millers, a minor league hockey team, played. The building really had atmosphere. It seated about five thousand fans. There were glassed off sections where the reporters sat and took pictures of the games. Below the rink were locker rooms and showers where the teams dressed for the games. I always sat in the center section so I could get the best view. I stood up and cheered when our team skated out onto the ice. I looked up to the senior hockey players and longed for the day when I would make the team. I hoped and prayed that some day I would be a Roosevelt varsity hockey player. However, I knew that it was a long shot because so many kids tried out for the team.

Terry, Bruce, and I had our old line together and played first line on the sophomore team. We did very well and won the city championship for the sophomore teams. We even got to play our

97

last game against Patrick Henry at the Dupont Arena before a varsity game. All our other games were held outdoors. I couldn't believe it when I first stepped my skates onto indoor ice. It was smooth like glass. When I slid the puck a little, it almost scooted down to the end of the rink. I was used to hard outdoor ice.

There was one sophomore on the varsity team. His name was John Ramsey. He was a hot shot and could skate like the wind. He seemed to fly over the ice. His strides were smooth and powerful. I was kind of jealous of him and thought he was a puck hog. He didn't seem like a team player. He never passed the puck to other players but tried to do it all by himself.

The varsity coach, Bob May, had the sophomore team scrimmage the varsity on occasion. They really knocked us around and wanted us to know we were only sophomores. The amazing thing was, our line usually held our own against them. That really made them mad. Bob May began to notice us too. In fact, one day I was watching the varsity practice and heard him yell at the players for not hustling. He said, "If you guys don't get your butts in gear, I have a sophomore line that can move right in and this team wouldn't miss a beat!"

Wow! I couldn't believe my ears. I knew he was talking about Terry, Bruce, and me. We could play at the varsity level. The coach was even thinking about us. Maybe that's why the players were so rough with us. We were a threat to them! However, we never did get a chance to play in a varsity game that year.

Waldo

In high school my friends pretty much stayed the same, with the exception of a few new ones who had similar interests. I rarely saw Bruce anymore. His friends ran in a completely different circle. However, it was strange how, when we did get together on occasion, both groups merged very well. I liked Bruce's friends, but they just chose a different lifestyle from me. His friends were the cool 'in group' kids. He was the natural leader, and everything revolved around him. He had a car now. He always had a girlfriend too, usually the cutest one in the school. All the girls liked him. There also were parties, booze, and cigarettes. Bruce had been smoking and drinking for quite a few years, and I hoped it wouldn't catch up with him. I only saw him drunk once. It was pretty scary.

We were still friends and respected each other. We just didn't hang out together. It was funny how we always felt comfortable around each other though. I think our childhood friendship was so deep that there would always be a bond between us. We just walked two completely different roads. When the roads merged, as they did on occasion, we walked together as friends. We were never jealous of each other and always pulled for one another. There was kind of an unspoken deep chemistry between us.

Terry and I were also really close. We always got together at Sibley Park where some kind of action was always going on. Almost all our activities centered around sports. We played touch football, basketball, volleyball, and baseball. We threw horseshoes, worked together in woodworking classes, learned to play chess, and continually played ping pong.

During the summer the activities slowed down a little at the park. Terry, Waldo, and I went caddying almost every day. Waldo was a very interesting friend. He was short, thin, and wore glasses. His brown hair kind of stuck up in the back. He lived with his single mom and had seven brothers and sisters. He played hockey too. He did not have a very stable home life and liked to hang around with me. He was creative and always getting into some sort of mischief. He was also good at earning money doing anything he could, both legally and illegally. I owe my first paper route, caddying job, and job selling papers at the Gopher football games to Waldo. I remember trying to sell papers one day at Memorial Stadium and having very little success. I was a little nervous about yelling, "Paper! Get your morning paper with all the latest line-ups." Then, it began to snow. Everyone suddenly wanted a newspaper, not to read but to sit on. We sold out and even got free tickets to see a Gopher game!

Waldo also got me into a lot of trouble. I remember one time when we were in junior high school. He came over to my house one day and said, "Tom, do you want to make some money?"

"What do you have in mind, Waldo?" I asked.

"Do you have an old Boy Scout shirt?" he asked.

"No, I don't think so," I said.

"That's okay," he said. "I have two of them. All we have to do is go house to house collecting money."

"How do we do that?" I questioned.

"It's easy. All we do is put on the scout shirts and say we're collecting money for some scout pack. That's all. It's easy. I've done it many times before."

"But, what if we get caught?"

"Who's going to catch us? Come on, Tom. It's fool proof! Believe me!"

Reluctantly, I went along with this wild scheme knowing full well it was wrong. We put the shirts on and went from house to house asking for donations. I could not believe how generous people were. We collected a great deal of money. Just like he said, it was easy and fool proof. I always let Waldo do the talking. After collecting the money, we'd sit on the corner and divide it up. Somehow, I never really enjoyed the money we collected. I knew it was wrong, but it was so easy. We did this for a couple of weeks and had all sorts of money. I was struggling, but it didn't seen to bother Waldo a bit.

One night, when we were out collecting money, we rang the wrong doorbell. A man came to the door. Waldo said, "Would you like to make a donation to the Boy Scouts of America?"

"What's the donation for?" the man asked.

"For scholarships for summer camp," replied Waldo. He was always quick to come up with some phony answer.

"What troop are you fellows from?" asked the man. I was really getting nervous.

"One forty-nine," Waldo responded.

"Where do you meet?" asked the man.

"At the gym in Standish School," Waldo replied. My face began to flush as I heard Waldo making up those lies.

"And who is your scout master?" asked the man.

"Mr. Johnson," responded Waldo.

"Who are you boys? And what do you think you're doing? The scout master isn't Mr. Johnson! It's me! How dare you collect money in the good name of the scouts! I think you boys better step inside!" he said in a very demanding voice.

"Run! Tommy," yelled Waldo. We both took off as the man yelled for us to come back.

"The police will be looking for you boys."

I was really scared when I heard that. I lived in fear for about a month. I thought there would be a full investigation and Waldo and I would be arrested. It seemed to blow over eventually, and we never got caught. I never let Waldo talk me into doing anything illegal again, except gamble.

In spite of Waldo's shortcomings, I liked him a lot. He was a good friend and fun to be around. It wasn't necessarily all his fault that we got into trouble. I was no angel. I could have said "No" at any point, but I didn't. Later in our relationship, I didn't go for his wild, illegal schemes.

The Caddy Shack

I went caddying almost every day during the summer before my junior year in high school. Terry had a car and so did I. I got my driver's license after three tries to pass the test. Mom sold the Studebaker and bought a Nineteen Forty-Nine, blue, torpedo back Chevy. It was sharp looking with skirt covers on the wheels. Since Mom didn't drive, it was essentially my car. However, I had to take her to church, the store, and run errands for her. I didn't mind because I loved to drive. I always managed to pay for gas which was only twenty-eight cents a gallon then. I felt free and mobile.

I didn't get into much trouble mainly because of sports and my friends. Also, I didn't want to hurt Mom. Whenever we got into an argument, she would cry and say, "You're just taking advantage of me because you don't have a father!" I hated that and usually came around to her point of view.

Terry and I took turns driving to the caddy shack. We caddied at a beautiful country club in Minneapolis called the Minikahda Club. Many of the wealthiest people in Minneapolis were members at that club. It was located in South Minneapolis near Lake Calhoun. It had a beautiful clubhouse with swimming pools, tennis courts, and a magnificent eighteen hole golf course. I first went caddying with Waldo when I was in junior high. Caddying is carrying golfers clubs, helping them with club selection, and keeping track of their golf balls. It's kind of like being a slave for four or five hours. When I was younger, I caddied for one golfer. That was called carrying singles. In high school we carried doubles. We were paid six bucks a round plus tips. We almost always got tips if we did a good job. Eight to ten dollars a day was pretty good money for us.

Bruce also caddied, but not as regularly as we did. Usually Terry, Waldo, and I drove together. When we got to the caddy shack, we gave the caddy master our numbers. He put us on a list, and we would wait for our number to be called. The caddy shack was a small white building with two rooms. One room was just for the caddy master and was his office. He kept track of all the caddies and also sold candy and pop from that room. The other room was a bigger area the caddies could use. There was a large grassy area around the shack and a basketball hoop in the back of the building. Kids from all over the city came to caddy there along with five hundred caddies. The five hundred caddies were adults who caddied for a living. They were always put on the top of the list and were the first ones to go out in the morning. A lot of things happened at the caddy shack while we waited for our numbers to be called. I learned to play poker, lag dimes, and play all sorts of sports.

Usually everyone made some money from caddying every day. While we waited to go out, we played poker for nickels, dimes, and quarters. That was exciting for me, and I really got into it. A couple of times I lost my day's work gambling. I'm an impulsive person and things like that really excite me. Waldo gambled more than he caddied. He was a good poker player and usually won.

I met a guy there named Joe Feden. He was a year older than me and much bigger. We became good friends. He had a very high voice but was tough. I once saw him deck a guy with one punch because the guy made fun of his voice. Joe was the best gambler I ever saw. One day he said, "Tom, give me five bucks, and I'll turn it into ten for you." So I did. I held his money and watched him play. He would bluff and everyone would fold. If someone called his bluff, he would lay down a good hand and usually win. He won twenty dollars that day and gave me back my five plus another five.

Joe was also a very good golfer. On Mondays we could play at the course free. It was called caddy day. I guess the course wasn't very busy then. They let us play in appreciation for caddying at their golf course. Joe and I went out together. I hadn't played much golf and wasn't very good. Joe was incredible! He shot a thirty-three on the front side which tied the course record. I couldn't believe the shots he made. He one putted seven greens. I learned to love golf by playing with Joe on Mondays.

I also got into some trouble at the caddy shack. We were playing basketball against some guys from Central High. Central was a pretty tough school. Waldo, Bruce, Terry, and I stood four guys in a tough half-court basketball game. I guarded a guy named Steve Bloom. We pushed and shoved each other pretty hard. I drove in for a lay-up, and he took my feet out from under me. I landed pretty hard on my head. I got up slowly and said, "What did you do that for, Bloom?"

"Because I wanted to! " he said sarcastically.

"Well, if you do it again," I said, "I'll take your head off!"

"Why don't you just try it now!" he said.

I walked over to him while the guys put the basketball down and circled around us. We squared off and began throwing punches. He was a tough kid, and I knew I was in for a struggle. He caught me in the face with a pretty good left. I hit him in the stomach and then in the face with a left hook. We exchanged blows back and forth for about ten minutes. Finally, he hit me square in the nose and blood oozed out. I went after him and drove him into the bushes where we continued to exchange blows. His shirt was all ripped up, and my face was covered with blood. I didn't want to quit, but Bruce stepped in and said, "That's enough, Tommy!" Bloom had had enough too, and we stopped fighting.

Bruce took me into the bathroom and rinsed his hankey out with cold water. He said, "Put this on your nose and pinch it. It's bleeding pretty badly."

"I'm going to stop this bleeding and finish what I started."

"No, you're not! You're bleeding pretty bad, Tommy. Besides, you made your point. He won't mess with you again. I guarantee it! Tommy, he's a tough kid and you didn't back down a bit," Bruce said.

Bruce was right. I didn't have to fight Steve Bloom again. In fact, we became pretty good friends and even played against each other in hockey. It's strange how things work. I gained a little more respect from everyone, including Bruce, just for getting a nose bleed.

Terry and I made a lot of money that summer. We were even selected to caddy in the Walker Cup Tournament. That is a tournament with the best amateur players from the British Isles against the best players in the United States. It was a four day tournament. I caddied for an English golfer whom I barely understood. He was short and couldn't hit the ball as far as the other golfers, but there wasn't anyone in the tournament who could putt as well as he could. He was in a tough match with an American golfer, and I was pulling for him to win. On the fifteenth hole when I went to pull out the flag, I accidentally stepped on the American golfer's line and made a footprint on the green. The American golfer shouted, "What's the matter with you, Caddy? Can't you see that you stepped right on my line? You know better than that!"

There were hundreds of people in the gallery watching and listening to him yell at me. I got all red and wanted to crawl in a hole. What made matters worse, he missed the putt! He glared at me as we walked to the next green. My golfer from England won the match, and I was glad. We made eighty dollars for caddying those four days. That was a lot of money for Terry and me.

I got quite an education at the caddy shack that summer. Some of it was good, and some of it was bad. One thing I know for sure, my legs and shoulders got a lot stronger by walking eighteen holes every day with two heavy golf bags. That was as good as weight training!

High School Hockey at Last

When school began in the fall, I decided not to go out for the football team. I was kind of small, and there already was a great quarterback on the squad. Later, I was sorry about that decision. I thought it would be better to concentrate on hockey.

In late October the coach called the first hockey meeting. About forty players showed up and only eighteen would make the team. We had a new head coach. His name was Bob Johnson. He had been coaching in Warroad, Minnesota, which was a small town located on the Canadian border. I didn't know it then, but he was destined to become one of the greatest American hockey coaches of all time. He later coached Colorado College and Wisconsin. At Wisconsin he won two national championships. He later entered the professional ranks and coached the Calgary Flames and the Pittsburgh Penguins. While with the Pittsburgh Penguins, he won the Stanley Cup Playoffs, which is like the World Series of hockey.

Coach Johnson seemed nice and friendly, and he really loved the game of hockey. He was also a good story teller and related to kids very well. At the first meeting he said, "Welcome to the varsity tryouts. I'm your new coach this year. We don't have very many returning lettermen. I've talked with your former coach, and he said there is a lot of talent coming up. I feel we will have an excellent team." Then he said, "When I talk to the press, I'll say we will be very young and inexperienced. But, don't you believe what you read in the paper because I think we can win it all this year!" He really motivated and instilled confidence in his players.

Coach Johnson couldn't wait for the outdoor rinks to be flooded. So, he began practice at nearby ponds that were frozen over. He said, "Next week the natural ponds in Richfield will be frozen over. We'll begin practice at six in the morning before school." When we met at the pond in Richfield, it was still dark out. We worked on skating and conditioning drills. Then, he gathered us together to talk to us. Suddenly, the ice split! I thought we were all going under. We all scattered, but the ice held.

Tryouts were very difficult! I felt awkward and like I was learning to skate all over again. I didn't think I was doing very well and prayed I wouldn't get cut from the squad. He cut the team down to twenty guys and posted the names outside his door. Terry, Bruce, and I were still on the list. However, some very good friends of mine and excellent hockey players had been cut. I felt sorry for them but happy I was still on the team. Terry, Bruce, and I hoped the coach would keep us together. My brother had taught us to be unselfish players, so we knew how to pass to each other really well. Finally, Coach Johnson made the last cut. I made the team! So did Terry and Bruce. Needless to say, we were thrilled!

It was exciting the next day after school. We went down to the equipment room and got our stuff. We got breezers, socks, shin pads, elbow pads, shoulder pads, gloves, and our jerseys. I was number ten. I wanted to make that number famous!

We practiced at Sibley Park, which was great for Terry and me, for two hours every day. I loved to play so much that after practice I went home for supper, came back, and skated until the lights went out at ten o'clock. Sometimes Terry and I took our shoes out of the warming house and stayed until midnight. We were real rink rats. There was just something about being out in the cold air and skating that made us feel as free as the wind. And believe it or not, Terry and I worked up a sweat on the coldest nights.

Our hockey season began with the Preview. This was when all the teams in the city played at the Dupont Arena for one period.

The fans and coaches saw all the teams at once and made predictions on who would win the championship. Three seniors were on the first line. Bruce, John Ramsey, and I were on the second line. Terry was on the third line. Hockey is so fast that a good team needs three solid lines. Each line can only skate for a minute or possibly two before getting tired out. All three lines see action. I was thrilled to be on the second line because that meant I would get a lot of playing time. The only problem was John Ramsey! He was an excellent hockey player, but for some reason we never clicked. He thought he was much better than me and never passed me the puck. He played center and Bruce and I played wings. Bruce, however, could handle him and acted as kind of a buffer between us. I tried to make the best of it but always felt uncomfortable. Bruce sensed my struggle but never talked to me about it. He just helped me out when he could.

Our team looked great at the Preview, and the newspaper said we were the team to beat. The stands were packed, and I loved playing for a cheering crowd. When we got into our regular season, Vic Qualie, our senior right wing on the first line, was ruled ineligible because he had moved in from another school district. Bob Johnson called me into his office and said, "Tom, I'm moving you up to first line." I couldn't believe it! I thought he would have picked Bruce or John Ramsey, but he didn't. He picked me! This would be difficult because Bud Bercan and Ken Erickson were not only terrific hockey players but also very fast. I didn't know if I could keep up with them. Also, I didn't know if they would accept me.

At the next practice I worked out with the first line. Bud liked me and encouraged me which made me feel good. Our coach moved a senior to the second line, but Terry was still on the third line. He always worked hard and never complained. Wow! I had wondered if I would even make the team, and now I was playing on the first line with our two captains. I appreciated the opportunity Coach Johnson gave me, and I didn't want to let him down. We won our first two games easily. I even scored a couple of goals and one assist.

During Christmas vacation our team traveled four hundred miles by bus to play in a tournament against Warroad, Thief River Falls, Hallock, and Roseau. Roseau was the defending state champion and had an unbeaten thirty-eight game winning streak going. We traveled on the bus with a team from St. Paul. When we arrived in Roseau, we checked into a motel. I roomed with Terry. We won our first two games in the tournament. I was not only fitting in, but I was developing confidence. Our last night there we went against Roseau, the defending state champs. They were big and looked awesome. I really had the butterflies! Butterflies are when your stomach gets all churned up and your nerves are on end. They usually go away after the first hit. So, I always wanted to get hit early!

Our coach said, "This is probably the best team you'll face this year! But, I believe you can skate with them. Don't be intimidated and check them closely. If we keep the score close, then we can beat them."

We skated onto the ice. It was very hard ice and cold in the arena. We circled around the rink and loosened up. The fans were on their feet cheering. The place was packed. They sensed this would be an exciting game. Our line skated out to begin the game. Their first line was awesome. They were the top scoring line in the state the previous year. They were big and confident. The referee dropped the puck, and Roseau got it so fast I couldn't believe it. They fired shots at our goalie that looked like rockets! He stopped them all that first shift. I checked my man very closely and didn't want him to score. Although we were badly outplayed the first period, the score was still zero to zero! Our coach tried to pump us up in the locker room, but we knew this was one terrific team. As we skated out for the second period, the crowd gave us a cheer. They were good fans who knew their hockey. They loved a good game and even cheered us when we made a good play. They were used to seeing their team totally dominate another team.

Early in the second period, Bud passed me the puck. I skated down the right side of the rink. Their big defenseman forced me to the outside, and I put on a burst of speed. I could not make the turn, so I went around the net. Bud slipped into an open area, and I passed him the puck. He fired a shot which hit the upper corner. The red light went on. I couldn't believe it, we were ahead one to nothing. Bud skated over and gave me a big bear hug and said, "Great pass, Tommy! Great pass!"

This goal pumped our team up, and we each turned it up a notch. We were all playing above our ability, and the adrenaline kicked in! This happens once in awhile, and we call it our second wind! We began to press them, and they knew they were in a game! I loved it! We were holding our own with last year's state champs! We went into the locker room with a one goal lead!

During the third period they really came at us. They were not about to let this no name team from the cities upset their winning record. I've never been hit so hard in my life. I was flattened at the blue line and driven hard into the boards on numerous occasions. However, I wasn't hurt and kept coming out for more! The game was so intense, both teams began to tire. We held our lead until the last minute of the game. Then, their big right wing broke loose and fired a slap shot so hard that I only saw it hit the net. The light went on and the fans went crazy. Fortunately, he was not my man.

Our line skated out with forty seconds left on the clock. We lost the face-off, and they came charging down to our end of the rink. They fired four shots which our goalie, Larry Price, kicked out! He was playing great. There was a mad scramble in front of the net, and their center picked up the puck and fired it over all the bodies on the ice. It went into the net with just three seconds showing on the clock. We lost the game in the final seconds.

They came over and shook our hands. They said it was their toughest game all year! We lost the game, but earned some respect. I felt good because I played well. My confidence began to grow. I felt like an important member of this team. I was accepted by both my coach and teammates as one of the key players on the team. When we returned to the cities, everyone talked about our team. The Minneapolis Star gave us a big write up in the sports page. They talked about our gallant effort against Roseau.

I lived for hockey games. The fans packed the stands when we played at the Dupont Arena. We played on Thursday and Saturday nights. My family came to all my games. My mom, brothers, and sister all came and sat together. We also had great support from our school. The crowd always pumped me up to play my very best. After the games I went home and talked with my brothers about it for hours. They all played hockey too and later became great players for Roosevelt High. I was the one who set the stage though.

Hockey became my whole life. It gave me status, friendships, and recognition. I didn't get into trouble anymore. Hockey was good for me at the time, but it's never good to put all your eggs in one basket. That was a difficult lesson for me to learn later on in life. But right then, l enjoyed every minute of it! My only regret was that my father never got a chance to see me play.

The State Tournament

Our team finished the City Conference with a ten and zero record. We won the City and Twin City Championship. We went through the playoffs and were representing section five in the State Tournament. We practiced very hard to prepare for this spectacular event in Minnesota. Teams from all over the state traveled to St. Paul, stayed in hotels, and played before crowds of ten thousand screaming fans. The State Tournament took place in late February on Thursday, Friday, and Saturday nights.

On Wednesday morning our school held a big assembly during the first hour of school. Everyone was super excited! Our team was on the stage, and the cheerleaders were getting everyone worked up! Our coach, Bob Johnson, was the first to talk to the students. He walked up to the microphone and began speaking, "I really appreciate all the support you've given our team all year. We have a great group of kids on this team who play with their hearts. Your support and enthusiasm has helped motivate us to play our very best. We are going to go to the St. Paul Auditorium and bring back the championship for Roosevelt High. Let's hear it for our Nineteen-Fifty Eight City Champions!" He motioned for all of us to stand up. The student body broke into a thunderous roar. He then went and sat down as the band played our school song. Everyone sang their hearts out.

Next, the cheerleaders came to the microphone and

introduced the team members. We each had to say something to the student body. When they came to Bruce, they asked him how he felt about going to the State Tournament.

He said, "Pretty good!"

"How do you think you will perform?" asked one of the senior cheerleaders.

"I don't know," he responded. When he sat down next to me, he looked pretty shook up.

"Are you okay, Wakes?" I asked.

"I choked, Tommy," he said. "When she asked me those questions and when I saw all those kids, I got tongue tied. I just couldn't think! I didn't know what to say."

"It's all right, Bruce," I said. "I think everyone understands. Besides, you do your talking out on the ice anyway."

Just then I heard, "Will Tommy Hall please come to the microphone?" I stood up and could already feel my face getting red. Now I understood how Bruce felt. The cheerleader said, "Hi, Tommy! How are you doing?"

"Fine," I responded.

"What will the team be doing today?" she asked.

"First, we'll check into our rooms. Then, we'll have lunch and all the other teams will be there. After that, we'll have an hour workout. I guess there will be a banquet tonight. And hopefully, we can get a good night's sleep," I said kind of surprised at how smooth everything came out.

"Thanks," she said. "That gives everyone a pretty good picture of what you'll be doing today. We'll be thinking about you when we're working hard here in school!" Everyone laughed and I went back to my seat.

"You were great, Hall! Where did you learn to talk in front of a group like that?" Bruce said in amazement.

"I just got lucky, I guess."

After the assembly our cheerleaders led the school in a couple of cheers. The band played and everyone was excited. We got up and walked to the bus. The flag team held their flags and made kind of an archway for us to walk through. We loaded the bus while everyone was cheering and going crazy! The Minneapolis Police Department sent two squad cars to escort us to the St. Paul Hotel with their sirens on! We all felt like celebrities and were fired up. We got to the hotel and checked into our rooms. Bruce and I were roommates. We couldn't believe it! It was like a dream come true, and it was really happening.

We had lunch and a light workout that afternoon. That evening we put on coats and ties to attend a banquet. I had never eaten in a restaurant in my life. We began with a salad and then a steak dinner. It was delicious! After dinner John Mariucci, the coach of the Minnesota Gophers, talked to us. He congratulated us on our success and said there would be many college recruiters and scouts watching the tournament. A sport announcer from Channel Five also spoke to us and was very humorous. After dinner we had a short team meeting. Our coach wanted us to get to bed early. He said it was important to get a good night's rest.

Bruce and I went back to our room and got ready for bed. We went to bed, shut off the lights, and laid there staring at the ceiling.

"Can you sleep, Halsey?" he asked.

"No! I'm too pumped up. I've never been treated like this! Who would have believed it? Remember when we first went skating at Sibley Park. You skated right away, and I couldn't even stand up."

"Yeah, but you sure worked hard and made the first line. You've had a great season, Tommy!" he said reassuringly.

"You did too, Bruce," I said. "Tomorrow we'll be skating together again. Vic Qualie is now eligible and is skating with the first line. It'll be me, you, and Ramsey on the second line. I wish it was Terry, you, and me. I struggle with Ramsey, Bruce. He never passes."

"He'll be all right, Tommy. This is the State Tournament, and we all have to pull together."

"Well, at least we'll be together and I'll get the puck to you. Just like old times," I said.

"I'm the one who needs to get the puck to you, Tommy, the way you've been playing this year," he said. "Well, we'd better get some sleep so we'll have some energy tomorrow," he said as he rolled over in his bed. "Good night, Tommy."

"Good night, Bruce." I turned to my side, curled my hands under my pillow, and fell asleep.

The next morning we ate a nice breakfast with the team. Our coach got us together afterwards and gave us some final instructions. Finally, it was time for us to go to our game. We picked up our equipment bags and walked to the St. Paul Arena. It was just a block away from the hotel. When we were tightening our skates, some men from the Chamber of Commerce came in and told us they were our hosts for the tournament. They gave us a box of oranges to suck on between periods. This helps when your mouth feels like cotton after skating your heart out. As we sat waiting to skate on the ice, my stomach was jumping around like there were butterflies in it.

Our coach stood up and said, "This is it, boys! It's what we've worked for all year. There's no holding back. Everyone gives 100%."

We put our hands together and shouted, "Let's go!"

We walked out of the locker room and jumped out onto the ice. A roar erupted from the crowd as our fans all stood up and shouted. As I skated around the rink, I looked up at all the people. I had never seen so many people in all my life. I felt like I was on top of the world. All these people were here to see us play. After we warmed up our goalie, we skated back to our bench. The announcer introduced us individually as we skated to our blue line. We took off our helmets as the band played The National Anthem. Then, we skated back to our net and formed a circle around our goalie. Bud, our captain, said, "Guys, we've played South St. Paul before. They're a very good team, but we can beat them! Everyone give their best effort and don't anyone take any cheap penalties."

We broke up and skated to the bench. The first line went out as the game began. It was a hard fought game. Our teams were evenly matched. After two periods the score was two to two. At the end of the game the score was still tied. We went into sudden death overtime! We were all very tired and tried to catch our breath as we waited for overtime to begin. With three minutes left in the overtime, Bruce and I started up the ice. He passed to me, and I passed back to him. He went around a couple of players, and the crowd was on their feet screaming. He crossed the blue line and slid the puck back to me. I went charging toward the goalie, and their big defenseman came over to cover me. Just as he reached me, I passed the puck back over to Bruce. He was wide open and just had to push the puck into the net. Instead, he whirled around and shot it backhand. The puck hit the pipe and bounced out. There was a mad scramble in front of the net, and the referee blew his whistle. As we skated off the ice, Bruce was hanging his head. We sat next to each other on the bench. "Nice pass, Tommy," he said with tears streaming down his face. "All I had to do was push it into the net. I could have put us into the semi's," he said. Then, he began to weep.

I had never seen Bruce cry before. "It's okay," I said. "We'll get another chance." Suddenly, we heard a loud roar and looked up to see our red light on. South St. Paul had just scored, and we lost three to two in overtime. We were heart broken. We skated off the rink hanging our heads. When we got into the locker room, our coach stood up and said, "That was a tough break, but I'm proud of you! You gave everything you had, and it was a great game. You have nothing to be ashamed of!"

We went back to the hotel. Bruce and I went up to our room.

"It's my fault we lost," he said as I shut the door.

"No, it isn't," I said. "We win and lose together as a team. It's not one person's fault."

"But, Tom! It was a wide open net. It was so easy. Why did I try to get fancy and spin around to my backhand side?"

I tried to console him, but he would not listen to me and blamed himself for our loss. None of us slept very well that night. We were moved to the consolation round of the tournament because of our loss.

The next day we played St. Paul Murray. We beat them four to two. Our final game was against International Falls. It was a hard fought game. The score was tied before the final period. In the locker room the coach came over to me and said, "You're not doing anything but skating up and down your wing. I'm benching you this third period!"

I sat on the bench the whole third period. I knew the reason I looked bad was because John Ramsey would never pass me the puck. We won the game and the State Consolation Championship. I did not feel like I was part of the victory because I watched the whole third period from the bench. Right then and there, I made a vow to myself that I would not play with John Ramsey the next year. I didn't care if I had to play third line. I would not play with him!

I will never forget all the excitement of the State Tournament. It was an experience of a lifetime. The whole state of Minnesota gets caught up in the excitement of this statewide event. I was glad to be a part of it and enjoyed rooming with Bruce, even if it didn't turn out quite the way I hoped it would. After the tournament was over, I was pretty exhausted from all the energy hockey had taken. I decided not to go out for the baseball team. It was fun just going home after school and not practicing every night.

Trout Lake Camp

During the summer before my senior year, I did a lot of caddying again to earn extra money. I drove to the caddy shack with Terry and Waldo almost every day. I tried to save some money because I didn't want to work my senior year of high school.

In the second week of August, I decided to go to Trout Lake Camp for the last time in my life. This was a camp located in Northern Minnesota on a beautiful chain of lakes known as the White Fish Chain. I attended this summer camp every year from fifth grade to my senior year in high school. It was a week long camp from Saturday to Saturday. This week in the summer came to be one of my favorite activities of the year!

The camp was built on a peninsula next to Trout Lake with hundreds of feet of lakeshore. The water was crystal clear and very different from the city lakes because of this clarity. It was like swimming in a pool without the chlorine. The camp had a large dinning hall, recreation room, a chapel, cabins, and wash houses. The cabins nestled in the woods among the pine and leaved trees and looked like miniature log cabins. The camp also had a recreational area with a baseball diamond, soccer field, and a miniature golf course.

During this week I always felt rejuvenated. The atmosphere was so positive and the program so clean that I felt responsive and alive again. The program was always excellent, and the staff knew how to reach out to kids. I met many friends from all over the state up there. We renewed our friendships during that one

118

week every summer. I knew this was my final week at Trout Lake Camp because I would be graduating from high school. It was a perfect place for me to be because there were all kinds of recreation, and I made the most of them all.

We went to camp on school buses which left from our churches. I rode the bus with several of my friends from school and church. Upon arrival we immediately checked into our cabins. The camp always tried to make the High Teens experience the most special one of the year. My friends, John Scheibe and Bill and Bob Larson, were in my cabin. Bob and Bill were twins and very intelligent as well as athletic. We all got along great together. We threw our sleeping bags on our bunks and headed for the dinning hall.

"What do you think camp will be like this year, Halsey?" asked John as we walked toward the center of the camp.

"It should be a lot of fun this year!" I responded. "I hope they have a softball game with the campers against the staff. I think we can beat them this year!"

"There sure are some cute girls, Tom," Bob said. "Hey, the one with the long brown hair just gave you the eye!"

"Yeah, right!" I said.

"You know there's going to be a banquet this year, and we each have to get a date," said John. "It's kind of a big deal. So, let's each pick out a girl! Okay?"

We lined up for lunch and sat down at the table. Lee Kingsley, the camp director, stood up and gave the same boring speech that we had heard every year.

"Now, boys and girls, welcome to Trout Lake Camp. We want you to have a good time at High Teens Camp this year. Remember not to destroy nature. No peeling bark off of the birch trees and that type of thing. How would you like to have someone peel skin off of you?"

John looked at me and just rolled his eyes. "That speech hasn't changed in eight years," he said.

"At least he's consistent," I said.

We had a wonderful week at camp. I won the ping pong tournament, and we beat the staff in a softball game. We enjoyed the beach and swimming in the clear waters of Trout Lake. Our favorite time, however, was the campfires. Each night we walked to the campfire area, sang songs, and told stories around the campfire. About one hundred and fifty campers attended our camp. We all sat on logs that were terraced into a semi-circle around the campfire. The campfire was built on a stone platform out in the lake. Trees surrounded this area. It was a gorgeous setting and very peaceful. A staff member led the campfires with his guitar and really got us singing.

John, Bob, and Bill all found girls to go to the campfires with right away. I was the only one left who needed to find a date. When we got back to our cabin at night, they would talk about their girls. I was still a little shy and uncomfortable around girls. I did, however, want a date for the banquet.

On Tuesday night when everyone got back to the cabin after cleaning up for bed, we laid in our beds and talked before our counselor came in. John said, "I walked Mary to her cabin after the campfire tonight. She is really nice!"

"Did you kiss her good night?" asked Bob Larson.

"You know, it's funny that you should ask," he said. "We were walking back through the woods with the full moon shining through the trees. I grabbed her hand, and she interlocked with my fingers. She sure is easy to talk to. All of a sudden, we stopped and turned toward each other. I looked deep into her eyes."

We were hanging on every word. "Go on!" Billy said.

"I knew it was the right moment. I put my arms around her waist and kissed her."

"How was it, John?" Billy asked.

"Her lips were soft and moist," he said. "It was great!"

I just laid in my bunk and listened to John talk about Mary. It all sounded great, but I knew I wasn't quite ready for that experience. John was pretty comfortable around girls.

"Halsey, why don't you ask a girl to the campfire tomorrow night?" John asked. "I've been watching Martha. She has an eye out for you. She's really cute too!"

"I don't think so," I said. "I don't even know her."

"Well, get to know her, Tom," said Billy. "You're running out of time! Besides, you need a date for the banquet on Friday."

Everyone drifted off to sleep. I just laid there thinking about John and Mary. It seemed so easy for him. What was my problem with girls? Why was I so frightened of them? Finally, I drifted off too.

After breakfast as I was walking to the drinking fountain, I saw Martha. I knew her name because I had heard her girlfriends talking to her.

"Hi!" she said. "Where you going?"

"Over to get a drink," I responded.

"I am too! Do you mind if I walk over there with you?"

"No, I don't mind," I said.

"Where are you from?" she asked.

"Minneapolis," I said. "Where are you from?"

"Isle, Minnesota."

"Where is Isle, Minnesota?" I asked.

"I'm surprised you've never heard of it," she said sarcastically. "It's the biggest town on Millacs Lake." As she was talking to me, I noticed she was a very attractive girl. She was about five foot seven with long curly brown hair. She wore white shorts with a pink blouse. She had a bounce to her walk and was bubbly. She seemed fun to be around and made me feel at ease.

"What's your name?" she asked.

"Tom Hall."

"Have you gone to this camp before this year?" she asked.

"Yeah, I've gone every year since fifth grade," I said. "It's a great camp. I enjoy it a lot. I hope you like it too!"

"I do like it! This is my first year up here, so I don't know too many people though. I saw you playing ping pong. You're really a good player."

"Thanks," I said. "Do you play?"

"No, not really," she said.

"Well, I could teach you. That is, if you want to learn?"

"I'd love to," she said.

"I'll meet you down in the Rec room after lunch, and we'll give it a shot."

"You've got a date!" she said excitedly.

I watched her as she walked away. She was as smooth as Bruce was on skates. I couldn't believe I was going to teach her how to play ping pong. It all happened so fast, and I hadn't planned any of it.

At the dinner table I was so excited that I could hardly eat. I saw her sitting a few tables away. She was talking with some girls. She looked over at me, but I quickly turned away. I didn't say anything to the guys. After lunch I ran to my cabin and changed into some shorts and tennis shoes. I walked to the Rec room and checked out two ping pong paddles and a ball. I waited for awhile, but no one came. I thought she must have forgotten about it. I was walking back to turn in the paddles when I heard, "Sorry I'm late, Tom, but I had to clean up my table."

"Oh, that's okay," I said.

We played for about an hour. She had never played before but caught on very quickly. We laughed a lot and seemed to enjoy each other. After we were done I said, "Do you mind if I walk you back to your cabin?"

"That would be nice, Tom," she said.

As we walked to her cabin, we bumped into John and Mary. They were headed for the beach. "Hey, Halsey! Where are you going?" John said with a surprised look on his face as he glanced at Martha and then back at me.

"Hi, John. I want you to meet Martha," I said.

"It's nice to meet you, Martha," he said. "This is Mary. Hey! Why don't you guys get your swimming suits and meet us down at the beach?"

"Yeah," said Mary. "We'll wait for you, and we can swim together."

"Would you like to go swimming, Martha?" I asked.

"Sure, I'd love to," she responded.

"Okay," said John. "We'll see you at the beach in about ten minutes."

"John's a good friend of mine," I said to Martha as we walked away. "We go to the same school together. I hope he wasn't too forward. You don't really have to go if you've got something else to do."

"Are you kidding?" she said. "I love to swim. I'll meet you by this hill in five minutes!"

I ran back to my cabin and put on my swim suit. I put on a tee shirt and hung a towel around my neck. I walked back to the hill and saw Martha waiting for me. She sure looked good in a bathing suit, I thought.

We went to the beach and had a ball. Martha was a very good swimmer, and we swam out to the dock and dove off the board. We had fun with John and Mary. It was the first time I had spent any amount of time with a girl. I enjoyed interacting with Martha, John, and Mary. As we walked back to our cabins, Martha and Mary were ahead of us talking together while John and I walked behind them.

"You're sure a fast worker, Tom," John whispered. "Last night I asked you to talk to her, and you said I don't think so. The next thing I see is you walking her to her cabin."

"It just kind of happened, John. We were at the drinking fountain, then I was teaching her how to play ping pong, and then I walked her back to her cabin. I don't know how it all happened!"

"Well, Tom, she's really cute and she likes you! I always knew you'd be a ladies' man some day."

"How do you know? I mean, how do you know she likes me?"

"I can tell just by the way she looks at you. Mary thinks so too," said John. "Are you going to ask her to the banquet?"

"Do you think she'd go with me?" I questioned.

"I'm sure she would. Maybe you should ask her to the campfire tonight first. You don't want to move too fast you know!"

John took Mary's hand, and they headed for her cabin.

"They sure are a cute couple," said Martha.

"They just met at camp this week," I replied.

"They seem like they've known each other longer than that. They get along so well together. I really had fun today," she said.

"I did too! Thanks for the swimming lessons. I was wondering if you would like to go to the campfire with me tonight," I said. This was the first time I had ever asked a girl out. I held my breath as she looked at me for a few seconds.

"Sure, Tom. I would love to go the campfire with you tonight."

"Hey, that's great! I'll see you after chapel tonight."

I walked back to my cabin where John was already telling Bob and Bill about Martha. Bob said, "What did I tell you, Halsey! Didn't I tell you on the first day of camp that she had her eye on you!"

That night after chapel, I walked up to Martha who was talking to a group of girls. "Hi, Martha!"

"Hi, Tom!" she said. "I need to go back to my cabin and get a jacket before we go to the campfire. I'll meet you by the bell."

"Sounds great!" I said. "I'll be there!"

We met by the bell and walked down the path to the campfire together. She asked me a thousand questions. I loved talking to her. We sat close together on the bench and sang campfire songs. I loved to see the glow of her face from the campfire light! After we went back to our cabins, I felt wonderful. The guys wanted to

123

know about our evening together. Now, I had something to share as well.

"Did you kiss her good night, Halsey?" John asked.

"You know, that thought never entered my mind," I said. Then, I turned a little red because everyone began laughing.

I spent a lot of time with Martha the rest of the week. She was so easy to talk to, and she seemed to be able to open me up. We sat by the lake Thursday night after the campfire and threw small rocks into the water and talked.

"You know, Tom," she said, "tomorrow is our last night at camp."

"Yeah, this week has really gone by fast!" I said.

"I feel like I've really gotten to know you this week. Thanks for being so open and honest with me," she said. "There's one thing you didn't tell me though."

"What's that?" I asked.

"That you are a big hockey star at Roosevelt High School!"

"Who told you that?" I questioned.

"I've got my resources," she said with a gleam in her eye.

"Well, we went to the State Tournament this year, but I am not a star."

"That's not what I've heard," she said. "You know, you are so modest. I've never met anyone quite like you before. I'm going to miss you, Tommy!" she said as she looked into my eyes.

"Martha, will you go with me to the banquet tomorrow?" I blurted out.

"I thought you'd never ask," she said. "Of course I will, you big dummy. Why did it take so long for you to ask?"

Friday blew by. We all got dressed up and ready for the banquet. I went to Martha's cabin. I couldn't believe it when she stepped out of the door. She had on a red dress and looked beautiful with her long tan legs and pretty smile. I stood there with my mouth open for a few seconds.

"Are you alright?" she asked.

"Yeah! Just a little speechless, that's all," I said. "I just can't believe that I'm going to the banquet with the prettiest girl at Trout Lake Camp. That's all!"

She walked over and gave me a hug. "You know, Thomas, you're something special!" she said.

We went to the banquet. Everyone in the camp was there. The

dining hall was decorated, and there were candles on each table. We had a wonderful meal and entertainment at the banquet. After the banquet Martha and I walked around the camp and talked and talked. I finally walked her back to her cabin. I stood and looked into her eyes for a long time. She looked back into my eyes. I said, "Martha, you made this week one of the most special in my life. Thank you!" She started crying.

"Are you alright?" I asked.

"You're so sweet and such a gentleman!. I don't want to say good-bye!" Tears were running down her face. I didn't know what to do. So I took my hanky out of my pocket and dried her face. I put my arms around her waist and drew her to me. I kissed her and held her tight. She kissed me back and squeezed me real hard.

"Good night, Martha! I'll see you in the morning," I said as I turned and walked toward my cabin. I walked about ten paces and stopped. I turned around. She was still standing there looking at me. I waved and turned and walked away.

It was difficult saying good-bye the next morning. We exchanged addresses. I watched her as she left the camp in a car. I waved as the car turned out of sight. My last year at Trout Lake Camp was special. I met a wonderful girl who liked me and treated me special. She helped me overcome my fear of girls. We wrote for a couple of months. Gradually, the letters stopped. I never saw Martha again, but I'll never forget that last week at Trout Lake Camp.

A Great Disappointment

After camp I walked down to the park. Terry was there shooting baskets.

"Where have you been all week, Tom?" he asked.

"I went to camp," I said. "I thought I told you that I was going."

"Yeah, I guess maybe you did," he said. "Did you hear what happened to Bruce?"

"No!" I said. "What happened?"

"Well, he and some of his friends went to a party in Wilmar. That's a small town about fifty miles southwest of the Twin Cities. There was a lot of booze there, and the party got out of hand. The police were called and Bruce, John Ramsey, and some other guys were arrested."

"What happened then?" I asked.

"They were taken to a police station. Bruce was asked to take a breath test. He blew into a balloon, and his breath tested a high level of alcohol content. The school was notified, and Bruce was ruled ineligible for all sports his senior year."

"That's terrible, Terry! Have you talked to him?"

"No. He hasn't been to the park, and I haven't seen him."

"What happened to John Ramsey?" I asked.

"He refused to take the test and wasn't convicted. He's still allowed to play."

"That sucks! That really sucks!" I said. "Bruce must be heart-

126

broken!"

"Didn't I tell you it would catch up to him, Tom? He was playing with fire and got burned!"

"I've got to talk to him!" I said. I walked home and called Bruce.

"Bruce, this is Tom calling."

"Hey, Tommy! How ya doing?"

"I'm doing fine, but I heard you're not doing so well."

"So you heard, huh! Well, I guess it's all over for me."

"Can I come and talk to you?" I asked.

"Yeah, sure. Come on over," he said. I drove over to his house. He came to the door and said, "Come on in, Halsey. No one is home." I walked into his house and sat on the couch. He told me the whole story.

"It was crazy, Tommy. Everything got out of control. The police pulled up, and I had nowhere to run."

"I heard Ramsey got off completely free!"

"Yeah, I guess he's got more pull than me," he said. "Oh well, more power to him. But, I want you to know that he was just as drunk as me."

"What are you going to do now?"

"I don't know! I guess I'll just party and get drunk and have a blast my senior year," he said with a far away look in his eye.

"Bruce, we would have had our old line together. Just like down at Sibley when we won the Midget Championship. It would have been you, me, and Terry. We had a shot at the State Championship. We'll never make it without you."

"You don't need me, Tommy! You're going to have a great year! If I go to the games, I'll sit on our opponent's side and cheer for you guys. If anyone says anything, I'll let him have it!"

"Bruce, I'm worried about you. They've taken away everything you love. You would have been the hero of the school this year. Please be careful and don't do anything foolish."

"I'll be all right! Maybe I'll still see you around school sometime. You take care! And thanks for coming over. You're the only one who has talked to me about this. My parents never even said a word to me."

I left Bruce's house with a sick feeling in my stomach. He lived for sports. Now, that was taken from him. It was his own fault, and he knew it. There was no holding him back now. I hoped he would stay out of trouble, but I was wrong.

I rarely saw Bruce during my senior year. He skipped school a lot and didn't come to any hockey games. I guess it was just too painful for him to watch us. I did see him at one very ugly scene, however. After the hockey games we gathered at Beek's Pizza Restaurant. Many kids from our school went there just to talk and have fun. It was known as the Roosevelt hangout.

One night as we sat eating pizza, some big guys from South High came into the restaurant. They were drunk and looking for trouble. I looked up and saw Bruce with them. They came over to our table and asked John Swartz to step outside. John was the biggest one at our table. He played on the football team and was tough but not a street fighter. One guy kept pushing John, so he finally got up and went outside. It was cold and snowing. The guy from South High, named Craig, had his head shaved and so did the rest of his gang. Bruce's head was shaved too. They were baldies. They wore Gant shirts, dress pants, and black wing tipped shoes. They were mean and tough street fighters. Craig began pushing John trying to goad him into a fight. John grabbed Craig, got him in a head lock, threw him to the ground, and got on top of him. Craig's buddies were drinking beer as they watched and standing in a semi-circle. We stood opposite them, and Terry was right next to me. All of a sudden, Craig reached into his pocket and slipped on the biggest pair of brass knuckles I had ever seen. He began beating on John's head and split it open. John let go of his hold. We moved in to help John, but Craig's friends broke their beer bottles and said, "Don't try it!" I couldn't believe Bruce was with those guys.

Craig stood up. John was holding his head and kneeling on the ground. Blood was running down John's face from the cuts in his head. Craig yelled, "Get up and walk!" John didn't move. Craig yelled again, "I said get up and walk!" Then, he kicked John in the face.

I was sick as I saw my friend being bullied and kicked in the face. We all wanted to help John but didn't want to get cut up with beer bottles. Finally, John stood up. Blood was pouring down his face and freezing on his skin. He looked terrible! A man from the restaurant came out holding a billy club. He said, "You'd better get out of here because I've called the police." Then, we heard sirens. Craig and his gang ran. The man helped

John into his restaurant. Terry and I went to our car. I was driving. I got in and Terry sat on the passenger side. Then, Bruce came over to our car. Terry rolled down the window, and Bruce hit him in the face.

Terry yelled, "Bruce! It's me, Terry! What the heck is the matter with you?" Bruce walked away in kind of a daze. I took off! As I drove home, Terry said, "Tom, can you believe that! Bruce didn't even know who we were!"

"I can't believe it either, Terry," I said. "Bruce is not a mean person. He's in big trouble. He's mixed up with the wrong crowd."

"I feel like such a coward, Tom!" said Terry. "We all just stood there and let that guy beat on John."

"Terry, those guys had broken beer bottles. They wouldn't have hesitated shoving them in our faces. It was an ugly scene, and I'm still shaking! Do you think John will be all right?"

"I hope so," Terry said.

On Monday I saw John in school. His head was bandaged up. He said he had twenty stitches in his head. I told him I was sorry we all didn't rush in and help. He said, "It's all right, Tom. My head will heal up. We were lucky that pizza guy called the cops. I shouldn't have stepped outside with those guys."

I didn't see Bruce much the rest of the year. He purposely stayed away from me. I heard he did a lot of drinking and partying. He was totally out of control now that sports were taken from him. He just couldn't handle it.

My Senior Year

Before hockey season started, I had gone to Coach Johnson's room one day after school.

"It's a tough break losing Wakefield," I said.

"Maybe, but he might have hurt us this year too, Tommy," he said.

"I don't think so, Coach. He's a great hockey player. He's a team player too."

"We'll just have to get along without him this year," he said.

"I don't want to play first line this year, Coach!" I said. "I know Ramsey is captain and will be playing first line, and I don't want to play with him. We just don't get along. I'm sure I'll do just as well on the second line. I'd like to play with Terry. We've played together for years down at Sibley Park."

"I know you and Ramsey don't get along. We need team unity. I don't want any dissension on this team, Tommy!" he stated.

"There won't be any dissension on the team. Just play Ramsey on the first line, and he'll be fine. I'm okay with playing second line. I'll get along with Ramsey just fine as long as I don't have to skate with him," I said.

"Usually, I don't like players telling me who they do and don't want to skate with. But, I know you love the game of hockey. I want you to give it all you've got because I think we'll have a great team and you're going to have a great year."

"Thanks, Coach! You won't hear me say another word about this to anyone."

We had a great season. I skated on the second line with Terry

130

Hall to Cooney, past the goalie and into the net for a goal.

and Billy Larson. We never started a single game, but we outscored the first line four goals to one. After the eighth game of the season, our team had eight wins and zero losses. John Ramsey was very jealous of me and would hardly talk to me. That was all right with me too. After the eighth game, I was the leading scorer in the city and Terry was second. Our biggest test was coming the next Thursday. We would play Southwest who was just half a point behind us. On Tuesday night I got very sick with a fever and skin infection. The coach came over to see me Wednesday night. When he saw how sick I was, he said, "Tommy, this is the worst break our team could have. We need you because you make our team go. You are our scoring punch. We'll have to change our entire line-up to play Southwest tomorrow night."

"I'm sorry, Coach. I wanted this game as much as you did! The guys will come through. You'll see!"

"You need to get well. We need you for the playoffs!" Then he said good-bye to my mom and walked out the door.

The next morning Mom brought in the morning paper. The headlines in the sports page read, "ILLNESS FORCES TED'S STAR OUT OF THE GAME." It was the first time I had ever been called a star. I was weak, but it was breaking my heart to miss that game. I called my friend Mike on the phone.

"Hi, Mike. This is Tom."

"Yeah, what can I do for you, Halsey?" he said.

"Are you going to the game tonight?" I asked.

"Sure am! I wouldn't miss it for the world. Boy, the team is sure going to miss you though."

"Could you do me a favor?" I asked.

"Sure! Name it!" he said.

"Call me between periods and tell me how the game is going."

"Yeah, I'll do that for you!" he said.

That night, sick as I was, I had an urge to get out of bed and go to the game. Mom would have no part of it. So, I waited for Mike to call. Finally, the phone rang and I answered it. It was Mike.

He said, "It was a pretty even first period and no one scored. The gamed is tied zero to zero."

"Thanks, Mike," I said. "Keep me posted!"

"We really miss you, Tom," he said. "The team seems flat without you!"

After what seemed like hours, the phone rang again. Mike was on the line again.

"It was an incredible second period. The puck never left our end. Larry Price, our goalie, was sensational. He wouldn't let anything through. The score is still zero to zero. It's like a different team without you in there. Our team is getting weaker, Tom. I hope we can hold on."

Finally, the final call came. Mike was breathing very hard. "We were badly out played," he said. "But, no one scored! The game ended in a tie! If Larry hadn't played out of his mind, we would have gotten killed. Please get well quick because we have no offense without you."

I couldn't believe we tied the game. I remained in bed for one more week. Slowly I began recovering from my illness. I began skating with the team in my sweats and realized I had lost some strength. I hoped and prayed I would be ready to play in the playoffs.

Tom Hall skates through Washburn players.

Our final game of the year was Patrick Henry. They had a good team but not a great one. We played them even in the first period. All we had to do was beat them, and we were in the State Tournament again. I still was not fully recovered, and the game ended in a one to one tie. I did score the tieing goal however. We also tied Southwest for the City Championship.

We won all our playoff games and were in the finals. Southwest was beaten by Central. We played Washburn in the regional finals to see who would go to the State Tournament. We had beaten them in a regular conference game five to nothing. The night of the big game came. I was fully recovered from my illness. There was a huge crowd of over five thousand people packed into the Dupont Arena.

Their coach had scouted us so they played us in a very tight defensive game. He put their top player on me. This guy followed me wherever I went. When the referee wasn't looking, he slashed at my heels and speared me with his stick. He wanted to goad me into a fight so we would both get kicked out of the game. We were losing. The score was two to one deep into the third period. Their star player had completely bottled me up.

With one minute showing on the scoreboard clock, the referee finally saw their player spearing me. He raised his hand and

133

called a penalty on him. Finally, I had that monkey off my back. Our team had a man advantage with one minute left in the game. We skated down to their end and peppered their goalie. One of their players iced the puck. I skated back and picked it up behind our net. I looked up at the clock and saw there was just twenty seconds left in the game. As I started up the ice, the crowd came to their feet. Everyone was screaming. I went around one player and then another. I was streaking down the right side of the rink, and the crowd was screaming, "Ten, nine, eight..." I knew I didn't have much time. Their big defenseman came charging out at me. I gave him a head fake and wheeled around him. I was bearing in on the goalie in the final seconds of the game when I saw a wide open net on the right side. I fired for the upper corner. The puck was heading straight for its target but just sailed over the net by less then an inch. The game was over! We were knocked out of the playoffs. I laid on the ice and wanted to die. I stood up and watched the other team pile on their goalie celebrating their victory. Their star player skated over to me. I doubled up my fist inside my glove and wanted to punch him. He took off his glove and said, "Nice game, Hall!"

I took off my glove and said, "Yeah, nice game."

I skated into the locker room. I was sick. My dream of going to the State Tournament as a senior was over. I couldn't even take off my equipment. Terry came over and unlaced my skates and pulled them off.

"If only that shot had been just an inch lower. He gave me the whole right side of the net. How could I have missed, Terry?" I said with tears in my eyes.

"It's okay, Tommy! You played your heart out!"

"So did you, Terry. I'll play with you any time anywhere!"

The next day we turned in our equipment. The season was over. It ended too abruptly. I was depressed and felt terrible. I thought if we made it to the State Tournament and I played well, I might get a scholarship somewhere, maybe even to the University of Minnesota.

The next week the paper came out with the All-City Team selection. I was named first team center on the All-City Team. I thought to myself, I'll bet this is the first time a second liner was named to the first line All-City squad.

Spring came very quickly after the hockey season. Before long we were practiccing for graduation. Finally, graduation night arrived. We all dressed in our caps and gowns. School was over. It was time for us to become adults and face the big bad world. I saw Bruce for a brief moment that night. He managed to graduate even though he got into all sorts of trouble.

I walked over to him. "Congratulations, Wakes!" I said.

"Yeah. Congratulations, Halsey!" he said. "What are you doing next year?"

"I'll probably be working. I don't have enough money to go to college," I said. "How about you?"

"I would like to go to college and become a teacher and a coach," he said.

"You're kidding," I said. "That would be great. I hope it all works out for you!"

"Hey, I'll see you around, man," he said as we shook hands.

After that moment we pretty much walked out of each others' lives. We bumped into each other on occasion and chatted briefly. However, our close childhood friendship did not carry over into our adult lives.

Senior Pictures

Bruce Wakefield

Tom Hall

Terry Cooney

Epilogue

Bruce never realized his dream of becoming a teacher and a coach. He went to college the next year. It didn't last though. He married his high school sweetheart at the age of nineteen. Shortly after, they had a baby girl. He had to work to support his family. Bruce became a carpet layer and now has his own business. He's presently living in a suburb of Minneapolis. He has raised four children. They are all adults now and have not married as of yet.

After high school I worked to help Mom out and save some money for college. One year later I enrolled at the University of Minnesota where I tried out for and made the freshman hockey team. I did very well, but my money ran out after one year. I dropped out of college to work again. The following year I enrolled again and put my full energy into my education. I graduated as an elementary teacher. I have been teaching for twenty-eight years and love working with kids. I've also done some coaching. I got married when I was still in college and six years later started my family. My son now teaches high school social studies and coaches hockey. My daughter is an elementary teacher. Both of my children are married.

I tell many stories about my youth to my students in the classroom. They encouraged me to write this book. I hope to write a few more in the future because this book only scratches the surface. Before beginning this project, I called Bruce on the phone.

"Hello, Bruce! This is Tom Hall calling." There was silence on the phone for a few seconds. I hadn't seen or talked to him in years.

"Tommy Hall, how are you?" he said.

"Fine! I'm calling you for a couple of reasons," I said. "First of all, I wanted you to know my mom died last weekend."

"Thanks, Tom, for calling. You know I deeply respected your mother. She was a great lady! She raised all you guys alone. When is the funeral?" he said.

"Next Wednesday."

"I want to come and pay my respects," he said.

"Thanks, Bruce! That's really nice and it means a lot to me. The second reason I'm calling is because I want to write a book about us growing up in the 1950's. I want to call the book Brucey Gravy," I said. "I want to see if your childhood memories are as vivid as mine." Once again there was silence on the other end of the line.

"Brucey Gravy, huh! Well, I'll be darned!" he said. "Yeah, my childhood memories are very vivid."

We talked for four hours. I couldn't believe it, but he remembered more than I did.

"You know, Bruce," I said when we were just about to hang up, "I idolized you as a child. You had it all. Everything was so easy and natural for you."

"And I looked up to you, Tommy," he said. "You had the strong family up-bringing with solid morals and values. I think we both had what the other person wanted. The difference is, Tommy, you're living out your dream and I never realized mine."

"I don't know if that's true," I said. "You're married and have raised four children."

"Yeah, but even with them I think I still blew it," he said. "I thought by coaching them in athletics that I could get close and bond with them. I was wrong because I never held them and told them how much I loved them. I hope they get married and have children. I'm going to be the best grandfather this world has ever seen. I'm going to hold my grand kids and tell them I love them all the time. None of my kids are married yet, and I'm hoping for one more chance."

I couldn't believe this was the tough Bruce Wakefield I once knew talking. When I hung up the phone, I had a wonderful feeling in my heart. I once again connected with my childhood friend. I wanted to tell the world our story.

———

About the Author

Tom Hall is a retired teacher from the Mounds View School District in New Brighton, Minnesota. He spent 31 years teaching and caring for 5th and 6th grade children.

Tom grew up in South Minneapolis in the 1950's. He is the third oldest of seven children and loved activity and action as a child. Tom loves all sports, but his favorite is ice hockey. He played as a child, in high school, and in college. He developed a love for children while working as a Park Instructor during his college years.

Tom has a Bachelor's Degree in Education from the University of Minnesota and a Master's Degree from Long Beach State College in California. As a classroom teacher, he taught three years in California, thirty-one years in Minnesota, and has had a full and rewarding teaching career.

Tom and his wife Sandy have been married for forty-three years. They have two children and ten grandchildren. Now retired, Tom is currently writing books, playing golf and tennis, spending time reading, and doing private tutoring.

Tom has great concern for teachers and tries to encourage, support, and help teachers as much as possible. He knows teaching is a difficult, challenging, rewarding, and fulfilling career.

Tom hopes to complete his life with the same energy he had as a child —with action, purpose, and activity.

39931356R00082

Made in the USA
Middletown, DE
24 March 2019